PRAISE FO
YOUNG ENTREPRENEUR

"They are Canada's most influential young entrepreneurs and I can think of nobody better to provide insight and inspiration to students of all ages. Swish and Quinn's entrepreneurial instincts and appetite are one of the many things that set them apart and their passion for giving back to the student community is unparalleled."
Tim Will Hyde, CEO of TWH Media

"Swish and Quinn have been inspiring young people around the globe for some time now. I couldn't think of a duo better suited than Swish and Quinn to write a book like this."
John Patrick Mullin, Co-Founder of MANTRA DAO

"Swish and Quinn are some of the best operators I know of any age. Their advice and anecdotes in *The Young Entrepreneur* are not just a must-read for people looking to build a business from scratch. They are also ideal for people who are looking to grow their personal brand and network."
Ravi Krishnan, Chairman and Founder of Stepathlon and Former Managing Director of IMG Sth Asia

"I love that *The Young Entrepreneur* not only dives into the ABCs of starting a business but also the intangibles of the journey: mental health, personal branding, networking, etc. It's truly a comprehensive guide for the aspiring entrepreneur!"
Dax DaSilva, Founder of Lightspeed Commerce

"It's a real treat that Swish and Quinn took the time to write down their perspectives, lessons, and advices in a book that will surely inspire and pave the way for the next generation of entrepreneurs."
Esther Vlessing, President of Canada Emergency Medical Manufacturers

"Swish and Quinn have the unique ability to take complex business topics and make it simple so that people are not only inspired but truly feel it is accessible to them. This book is truly a gift to the future generation of leaders."
Rachel David, Founder of Hashtag Communications

"Swish has consistently championed building a business while you're young and he's the best example of why anyone can do it. Entrepreneurship is an incredibly challenging path to take, but at the same time, the most rewarding thing one can do if they love creating opportunities and solving real problems. Swish's framework makes it easy for everyone to understand and get started."
Jason Wong, Founder of Pughaus

"Youth entrepreneurship is vital to any economy and I love that Swish breaks down in simple, easy-to-understand language how any student can start a business even if they are limited by time or money."
Manny Padda, Managing Partner of LOI Venture

"Entrepreneurship fosters a critical set of skills every young person needs – curiosity (about a problem space), ingenuity (to solve the problem), tenacity (in the face of challenges), empathy (for the customer), and storytelling (so the world understands what you're trying to do!). Through practical guidance and tangible stories, *The Young Entrepreneur* is a must-read!"
Cheesan Chaw, COO of RBC Ventures

"Entrepreneurship requires you to step into various roles at once. Building a product and growing a team is an experience that requires grit, determination, and resilience. While it requires you to take calculated risks, it is one of the most rewarding experiences. Quinn and Swish share practical steps and approaches to building a business from scratch. Sharing their knowledge will encourage and equip the next generation of young entrepreneurs globally. *The Young Entrepreneur* provides a foundational framework to building a business with meaning and purpose."
Ravina Anand, Co-Founder of FLIK

"Swish and Quinn's entrepreneurial pursuits began at a very young age, and I am continuously inspired by all that they accomplish. It is essential that we teach entrepreneurship to college students, so that they feel empowered to begin creating a positive difference in the world. Swish is the epitome of someone who didn't wait for others to tell him he was ready to begin making a difference – they just *did* it! We need more young people to follow in their footsteps."
Ann Makosinski, inventor and *Forbes* 30 Under 30

The Young Entrepreneur

How to start a business
while you're still a student

Swish Goswami
Quinn Underwood

KoganPage

Publisher's note

Every possible effort has been made to ensure that the information contained in this book is accurate at the time of going to press, and the publishers and authors cannot accept responsibility for any errors or omissions, however caused. No responsibility for loss or damage occasioned to any person acting, or refraining from action, as a result of the material in this publication can be accepted by the editor, the publisher or the author.

First published in Great Britain and the United States in 2018 by Kogan Page Limited

Apart from any fair dealing for the purposes of research or private study, or criticism or review, as permitted under the Copyright, Designs and Patents Act 1988, this publication may only be reproduced, stored or transmitted, in any form or by any means, with the prior permission in writing of the publishers, or in the case of reprographic reproduction in accordance with the terms and licences issued by the CLA. Enquiries concerning reproduction outside these terms should be sent to the publishers at the undermentioned addresses:

2nd Floor, 45 Gee Street	8 W 38th Street, Suite 902	4737/23 Ansari Road
London	New York, NY 10018	Daryaganj
EC1V 3RS	New York, NY 10001	New Delhi 110002
United Kingdom	USA	India

www.koganpage.com

Kogan Page books are printed on paper from sustainable forests.

© Swish Goswami and Quinn Underwood 2022

The right of to be identified as the authors of this work has been asserted by them in accordance with the Copyright, Designs and Patents Act 1988.

ISBNs

Hardback	978 1 7896 6036 4
Paperback	978 0 7494 9734 7
Ebook	978 0 7494 9733 0

British Library Cataloguing-in-Publication Data

A CIP record for this book is available from the British Library.

Library of Congress Control Number
2022934099

Typeset by Integra Software Services, Pondicherry
Print production managed by Jellyfish
Printed and bound by CPI Group (UK) Ltd, Croydon, CR0 4YY

This book is dedicated to our family, friends, mentors and, most importantly, Bilal Saleemi. We would not have been able to put this out without all the support we have received over the years. Love you all!

CONTENTS

LIST OF TABLES

ABOUT THE AUTHORS

Swish Goswami

Swish Goswami, 25, is the CEO of Surf, a tech company giving brands a better way to engage and understand consumers while compensating consumers for their data. Surf's revolutionary browser extension passively rewards people for their everyday browsing and helps them save when shopping with their favourite brands. Surf's brand division provides high-fidelity data and commerce enablement opportunities to some of the world's biggest brands such as Netflix, NBA, Sony Music, L'Oréal and Electronic Arts. Surf's vision is to build an equitable data economy and the company has made two acquisitions and raised millions from several NBA players, unicorn founders and venture firms.

Swish has given three TEDx talks and is an investor/adviser through his angel fund AGEX Capital in companies such as FaZe Clan, Wombo and Upstream. He has a personal following of over 200,000 and enjoys speaking around the world under North America's prestigious bureau Speakers Spotlight. For his entrepreneurial and philanthropic achievements, Swish was inducted into Plan Canada's Top 20 Under 20, recognized as LinkedIn's Top Voice and Startup Canada's Young Entrepreneur of the Year and awarded the United Nation's Outstanding Youth Leadership award.

Quinn Underwood

Quinn Underwood, 25, is the CEO of Autumn, a privacy-first platform that leverages AI to help users passively measure and manage their mental health in real time through analysis of digital behaviour. Because what you can't measure, you can't manage. His company has raised more than $2 million in venture capital from some of the top VCs in North America, and works with many of the fastest-growing companies in North America.

Previously, Quinn was a co-founder of ADVIN, a health-tech company he co-founded and helped scale across Bangladesh and India. During his time there, he helped grow the team to more than 20 employees, and served more than 150,000 patients, while in his second and third years at the University of Toronto.

FOREWORD

Innovation comes from iteration. Back while I was pursuing my undergraduate degree at Queen's University I noticed a gap in the market, so I decided to create North America's first zero-waste consumer coffee shop. Being in the sustainability business taught me the importance of being scrappy, resourceful, and that constraints actually create creativity rather than reduce it. Our Tea Room café was picked up by the national press for being both progressive and innovative.

Upon graduating I decided to start a caviar fishery with two of my friends, Anatoliy Melnichuk and Ryan Marien. I distinctly remember driving to New Brunswick in Ryan's Toyota Camry. Atlantic sturgeon were in scarce supply, and New Brunswick was one of the few remaining places you could catch them, but you needed a licence that we didn't have.

There were five retired local fishermen with licences to fish sturgeon. After a 10-hour wait outside the house of one of the fishermen, we caught him for a quick conversation about using his licence and boat that summer, and he agreed. Evandale Caviar was born and nothing could stop us.

Except the massive market crash in 2008. Our thesis had been right; chefs couldn't find quality caviar consistently and we had no problem selling it to them when things were good. However, caviar tends to be the first thing restaurants remove from their recipes in a recession. Our luxury food startup was going to be eaten alive. This really taught me the importance of timing.

For our next venture, we applied what we had learned from New Brunswick fishermen to a new industry and created an e-commerce platform called Buytopia. It was eye-opening to me that it was possible to get 2.5 million users, acquire and integrate seven competitors and become one of Canada's fastest-growing companies with zero external financing.

After that we launched SnapSaves in 2013 – a mobile savings platform that gave you cash back for everyday purchases. Less than a year later, SnapSaves was acquired by Groupon. I am often asked how I was able to grow SnapSaves from idea to acquisition in eight months. My answer is always the same: I didn't. SnapSaves was an overnight success that was a combination of eight years of consistent hard work, constant innovating, and endlessly iterating on new business ideas.

There is no perfect time to start a business. You need to take a leap of faith and let the vision you have for your company guide your decision making. The fear of starting is there regardless of what age you are so why not start early? As a young entrepreneur your superpower is speed. Take your idea to market as quickly as possible and listen to feedback from early customers. Larger competitors can't compete with you on speed. You own the advantage of being able to iterate your idea, test and repeat it again before bigger competitors can even start.

Focusing on being fast, having a growth mindset and not being afraid to try new things helped keep me motivated along the way of my own founder's story. When I look back on my own companies, and after hearing countless founder's stories on *Dragons' Den*, I noticed that every entrepreneur's experience is unbelievably unique but they all had at least one shared struggle in common: access to capital. It was this insight that ultimately led me to create Clearco.

Today, Clearco gives founders the funding they need to grow without taking any ownership of their company, charging interest or requiring personal guarantees. As a young entrepreneur it's extremely difficult to raise money without giving up equity. Founder dilution is at an all-time high. At Clearco we believe there's a more founder-friendly way for funding your company compared to capital from banks or VCs. By being unbiased and using your company's data, we're able to be faster and fairer than any other form of investment. Founders often think it's too good to be true that you can access up to $10 million within a day or two of talking to us.

Much like this book, Clearco was created with one mission in mind: to help founders win. Our company is built for entrepreneurs, by entrepreneurs. And I can confidently say that we're well on our way to accomplishing that mission. We've already invested almost $1 billion into 2,200 companies. I attribute a lot of that success to optimizing for speed and execution and striving for done instead of perfect.

As a student you're told that you should aim for 100 per cent on a project and that's the quintessential benchmark for success. However, entrepreneurship provides a stark contrast to this. As a founder, you need to prioritize speed. In order to do that, you will need to get comfortable with the idea of putting a product to market that's only at 60 per cent. I believe that there is a lot of value in students developing an entrepreneurial mindset and being at the forefront of the innovation economy. The more entrepreneurs we have, the more disruptive we will be as a country. If you are the kind of person that learns by doing, there is no better way to learn entrepreneurship than to start a business for yourself.

Along the way, you will feel hopeless, lonely and confused. And that's completely normal. Use this book as a manual when you get these feelings. I've had the pleasure of knowing Swish for a few years now and am an investor in his company, Surf. I have had the opportunity of watching him blossom into an excellent entrepreneur and an even better person. I'm so proud of the work he has done to date in his career and have no doubt he will continue to crush it. He is an inspiration for young entrepreneurs everywhere, because he iterated on an idea and had the courage to pursue it. Swish understands first-hand what it takes to navigate the difficulties of entrepreneurship and he regularly champions the issues that young people experience in society today. I hope you enjoy reading this book as much as I did, and I hope this book makes you realize that the world is truly at your fingertips. All you have to do is start.

Michele Romanow
President of Clearco and dragon on *Dragons' Den*

Introduction

We can't bear the inauthenticity of traditional business books that make formulaic claims about 'quick and easy steps to becoming a millionaire' or the 'six easy steps to make your business boom'. That's not what this book is about. We're here to tell our story, convince you that you're entirely capable of being the person at the head of a brilliant and successful company, and to give you advice on what we found works and what doesn't based on personal experience, and the vast insights of all those we look to for mentorship and advice.

Our aim in the following pages is to cut through the noise surrounding entrepreneurship, to make a clear case for starting your own company while you're young and how to go about doing so. To be frank, there's a lot of misinformation that is regularly propagated in the media when it comes to entrepreneurship. We're here to offer a more realistic perspective than you might find elsewhere. Capital-E Entrepreneurship is not riding around in private jets or making money on a beach in the Bahamas; it's a lot less glamorous than that. A lot of an entrepreneur's life is in the trenches, at the office alone, working on a dream while friends are out without you. We don't say this to be discouraging, but to be realistic. And that isn't to say that those things can't be vastly rewarding, or even fun. Entrepreneurship offers a number of incredible benefits, that for many are enticing enough to divert them from the traditional career path. Entrepreneurship offers the freedom to set your own agenda, to have an impact on the communities you care about, and the opportunity to be audacious. What we aim to do here is provide you with the tools you need to build your company and to help you to better anticipate and bear the chaotic workload and the sacrifices that come with it. Both of us began our foray into entrepreneurship at a young age, and we think business and the world in general stand to benefit from further youth involvement. That's why we wrote this book.

We wrote this book with a great sense of responsibility. Never before has the world faced so many incredible challenges, from climate change to increasing political polarization, from voter apathy to nuclear brinkmanship. Our generation, whether we like it or not, must tackle these issues head-on. We have no alternative, we must work to make this world a better and more livable place like our lives depend on it – because in many instances, they do. But this doesn't have to be a burden; it is exciting, it is freeing, we have a purpose. Steve Jobs once said, 'everything around you that you call life was made up by people that were no smarter than you and you can change it, you can influence it, you can build your own things that other people can use. Once you learn that, you'll never be the same again.'

With every recommendation we make we'll also provide a concrete example illustrating how we, or other incredibly experienced businesspeople, came to that conclusion. With each chapter, we'll walk you through how we approached that topic in our own businesses. This book is about being practical and authentic. Both of us are entrepreneurs, and in the process of writing this book we were busy applying the very skills and advice we included in the following pages to our own companies. For Swish, that means Surf, the world's leading audience analytics platform helping brands engage and understand consumers while compensating them for their data. For Quinn, that means Autumn, a platform to help individuals and organizations quantify psychological well-being using artificial intelligence. We're here writing this book because we've built companies and we wish we had initially had a better understanding of how to go about doing so, and more importantly, how to go about doing so as a student, with all the advantages and disadvantages that come with that. We have also interviewed several successful entrepreneurs, many of whom are between the ages of 18 and 25, to ask them what about their high school and/or college careers helped them develop an entrepreneurial mindset to tackle some of the world's biggest problems.

This book is split up into three broad sections: entrepreneur, endeavour, and ecosystem. In the first part, you'll learn how to think like an entrepreneur and manage the stress and responsibilities that come with the job. Part Two will focus on the endeavour and will break down everything from how to get started with an idea to how to take that business and sell it. Finally, Part Three will speak to your role as an entrepreneur in a broader ecosystem and how you can go about being a greater part of it.

Part One
Entrepreneur

01
The entrepreneurial mindset

Don't worry, this isn't our attempt to break into the self-help industry – but we've definitely found that mindset matters. Actively and conscientiously incorporating these perspectives into your daily routine will make you a better leader and, frankly, a better person. The following list is an attempt to identify the various characteristics and practices common amongst the entrepreneurs we've had the pleasure of learning from and working alongside over the years. It's by no means exhaustive – there are many types of successful entrepreneurs with various strengths and qualities, some of which are stated here.

Audacity

We are by many measures the last generation capable of preventing global catastrophe, and for it, we must have the audacity to take on solving the world's most pressing issues; there are no second chances left. That audacity, it is a moral imperative for all those able to recognize and act upon the injustices so many still face – to make your voices heard, to make your actions felt, to confront those who have chosen ignorance and complacency and over justice.

That dramatic monologue was one Quinn delivered to delegates from more than 190 countries at the One Young World Summit in 2019 in The Hague, Netherlands during his last year of university. As you may have noticed, he enjoys a touch of drama, but don't let that diminish the significance of what he was trying to say. This generation is certainly faced with not just one, but many daunting and seemingly impossible tasks. Tasks that demand audacity if they're to be solved. You'll need that very same audacity in starting a business, and hopefully, starting a business to solve these global problems. Audacity is the willingness to take bold risks. Starting a company demands this – statistically nine out of every ten startups fail.[1] In order to be successful in starting your own company, you need audacity, a willingness to make a difference. This is not a call for recklessness, action without careful preparation or thought. Nor is this a 'you can do anything you set your mind to' moment. This is us telling you that if you're going to start a company, there's no point in aiming low. We're here to help ensure that when you aim high, you have a better idea about how to get there. You don't need to have every person sign an NDA before you tell them your ideas, because it's never an issue of ideas. It's an issue of execution. In order to execute on your ideas, you need to be audacious. Audacious enough to commit to turning your idea into a reality, challenging yourself to take a risk.

Taking initiative

There are countless ideas in the minds of countless people, many of them with the potential to change the world. Most of those ideas never see the light of day. Motivational posters worldwide read 'The best time to plant a tree was 25 years ago, the second-best time is today.' Most people just end up collecting a whole lot of seeds. This happens for a variety of reasons: people may not be able to find the spare time to explore their idea, or maybe they don't have the money, or maybe it would mean giving up a certain amount of financial security, or entering a field they don't know much about. The reasons are endless, many of them entirely valid. It's hard to do new things!

One of the most important characteristics of any entrepreneur is the willingness to take their ideas and act on them, even if it's just in some small way; whether that's cold-emailing a professor or expert to ask them a question, or taking it upon yourself to start a club, social movement, magazine, small business, or any other medium by which you have an aspiration, and working to make it a reality in some way. That willingness to take initiative makes all the difference. It's not an innate tendency either, it's largely socialized! When those around you are busy starting clubs, growing social movements, or building companies, it's far easier to do the same. That's partially why this book is focused on youth, and in particular those in school, be it community college, university, high school, graduate school, or anything in between. Contrary to popular belief, **being in education presents you with the perfect environment for starting your own business.**

You're surrounded by people exploring the limits of human knowledge, pushing to better themselves, and bringing their ideas to life. It's a great environment for not only inspiring new ideas, but also acting on them, and that makes all the difference.

The three 'whys'

Any entrepreneur will tell you that in order to become successful, you must be critical of the world we live in. Critical not in a disapproving sense, but an analytical one. As an entrepreneur you're constantly looking for problems to solve – because when you start asking questions no one else is asking, you start getting answers no one else has. That's when things get exciting.

A simple way to make a habit of this practice is to ask 'why' three times in a row after any question you pose to yourself. Every time you say or think 'why', do so two more times, challenging each answer you arrive at. Even for questions as trivial as 'why isn't it clear whether this door requires me to push or pull to open it?' (this is a real issue known as Norman Doors – seriously, look it up).

The point of this practice is to cultivate a more critical perspective of why we do the things we do. There's always a reason, and it's almost always more interesting than you think. The world is an incredibly complex place, and when we forget that, it becomes a little less bright. Relish the complexity, for in that complexity is endless opportunity for improvement.

Perhaps you knew all of this already, or perhaps you didn't. Either way, it's a simple exercise that only requires curiosity about the world around you and a few online searches. The benefits of this practice will make themselves increasingly clear in future chapters.

Responsibility

As the founder or leader of any company, you're charged with an incredible amount of responsibility. Everyone knows that, and we're not here to repeat the obvious (ignore that we just did). The responsibility we're talking about is the responsibility to improve the world around you. We don't mean social justice save-the-pandas stuff (although that wouldn't be all that bad either). We mean the profound responsibility we have as youth, as the next generation of world leaders, industry leaders, voters, and change-makers, to contend with the existential challenges we face as a global society. Jobs face massive disruption through AI, global warming threatens to cause 250,000 additional deaths a year by 2030,[2] and between 200 and 500 million people could become displaced by 2050.[3] These are not trivial issues, and they stand to affect our generation more than any other. All of us as youth have the opportunity to make a real difference in solving these issues. We would contend that at the very least, given that opportunity, we have a responsibility to try solving them.

Nevertheless, this is a book about how to start a business, so here's the business case for building a social enterprise.

The first thing you're going to do as an entrepreneur is identify a problem. The bigger the problem, the bigger your market, and the bigger your market, the bigger your potential value as a company. When you go to potential funders, whether it's venture capital or your next-door neighbours, you're going to have to explain to them why people or companies are going to buy your goods or services and why they should give you money. As will be illustrated later, the more salient the problem, the easier selling your solution becomes. Being able to say that your solution is going to save their jobs, their lives, or their homes makes for a pretty solid pitch. It's smart business.

Second, with talent as an increasingly limited resource, incorporating social impact into the core of your business provides an advantage when attracting the best talent. Studies show that 82 per cent of youth say it's important that a company actively considers its social impact.[4]

Third, your story and brand will become a foundational aspect of your company as you grow, with implications for everything from investment, to talent attraction and retention, to scalability. Focusing on social impact as well as profit positions your business narrative in a way that is broadly accessible to your customers, and positions you well for media coverage in the future. A successful business, particularly one focused on individual consumers, is as much about how you make your consumers feel as the quality of the service or good you provide them (this is part of why Apple is able to get away with charging people far more than its competitors). Doing so in an *authentic* way is a brilliant method for differentiating yourself from competitors and maximizing your reach.

Social problems: the foundation for entrepreneurial ideas

Both of us have spent a lot of time thinking about what we could be doing better as a society, so we provide you with a list of what we and others see as the world's most pressing problems. While this may be oddly placed for a book on entrepreneurship, we think bringing these questions to the forefront of the conversation is important if you're to be the future industry leaders and disruptors who, whether explicitly or implicitly, will be solving or perpetuating many of these problems with the businesses you build. Facebook or Twitter never planned on sitting in front of the US Senate answering questions around privacy or freedom of speech, yet the decisions they made early on and the business models they rely upon have played major roles in driving the societal dialogue around these matters. Thinking about these global issues as you embark on your business can make all the difference in the impact you have as you grow.

Work

The future of work is an unknown one, wherein three major problems have been identified by experts: rising rates of worker precariousness as the gig economy grows; the growing divide between remote and physically co-located workers; and the need for workers to be retrained as automation becomes more disruptive. The future of work is also an issue in the forefront of corporate minds because of Covid-19 and the dramatic changes people have seen with their workplace and work expectations.

Privacy and freedom

Two major conversations under the umbrella of freedom demand further consideration: the issue of privacy, and an issue of speech. As Big Data becomes more valuable with the increasing capabilities of our software and hardware, companies and governments will become increasingly keen to collect individual data. How will we protect our privacy? What's worth protecting? What kind of data can we consent to providing companies in exchange for goods and services? How can we value people for the data they provide? The second conversation is on freedom – what freedoms are we going to protect and how? Freedom of speech is one of our most fundamental rights, and deciding which limitations are necessary is fundamental to any platform that allows for open communication and collaboration, as many social media platforms do.

Inequality

Inequality exists across all possible distributions of goods and states; some of the most concerning, including income inequality and health inequality, have soared in recent decades. Historically, massive income inequality such as what exists now has only ever been addressed through natural catastrophe or war, neither of which are attractive solutions. Solving these inequalities through redistribution, technological improvement, or changes to the systems and structures that drive them are crucial to ensuring that peace and stability reign in the coming decades. Understanding the drivers of these inequalities offers ample opportunity for innovation and social change.

Immigration

Concerns over immigration have only worsened in recent years as populism has dominated political processes internationally.

Understanding the concerns at the heart of anti-immigration and pro-immigration rhetoric is necessary if they're to be addressed. The world is set to see massive increases in statelessness, with up to 500 million individuals stateless (forced from their homes) due to climate change and war by 2050.[5] Leveraging new technologies and approaches to help mitigate the drivers of statelessness and abate fears around immigration is crucial to ensuring the safety and well-being of the not-so-distant future.

Nationalism

Nationalism has dominated recent discourse around identity, and while not inherently harmful, can become so if unchecked. Rethinking how we consume information and discuss identity is ripe for innovation and disruption as younger generations enter broader society and its institutions.

War

The *Bulletin of Atomic Scientists* is in charge of adjusting the 'Doomsday Clock', a clock designed in 1947 to reflect the likelihood of nuclear Armageddon and the end of humanity. Scary stuff. It's important to note that the clock is no definite measure, but a perceived reflection of the state of the world and the possibility for nuclear war as judged by a group of atomic scientists. The clock started at seven minutes from midnight and has fluctuated between 12 minutes and its all-time low of 100 seconds. It was determined in 2020 that the clock 'is now 100 seconds to midnight'.[6] The causes that drive this assessment include the perception of science by powerful figures such as the US president, the rise of populism, climate change, or the possibility of cyber warfare.

All of these factors demand our attention, and the innovations of our generation will play an important role in increasing or decreasing these global risk factors. Some experts suggest that the next great war will be a cyber one. Cybersecurity is in dire need of our devotion and innovation. As more and more devices enter the Internet of Things, the security of our cyber systems becomes more precarious. The next weapon of mass destruction could be a fleet of autonomous cars hacked to target critical infrastructure and individuals, or it could be a smart toaster. The point being, there exists broad consensus that the security of our increasingly connected world is not where it should be – it's on us to change that.

Truth

What is true and what is not? Agreeing to a basis of fact is profoundly important to promoting a culture of informed and rational discussion shaping how we solve our problems. In an age of digital siloization and viral misinformation, it's crucial that we evaluate *how* we evaluate more closely, promote truthful information, and balance information consumption. With media platforms engineered to maximize virality, it's crucial that we better equip ourselves to distinguish fact from fiction. Recent innovations include the ability to identify fake news and better understand how it spreads, alternative social media platforms that promote more thoughtful interaction, and much more.

Climate change

The 2018 report by the Intergovernmental Panel on Climate Change (IPCC) illustrated the profound harms of human-driven climate change, citing the total destruction of all coral, increases in extreme weather events, heatwaves that render regions almost uninhabitable, and rising sea levels that threaten hundreds of millions worldwide living in coastal regions. Leveraging not only policy change and fossil fuel reduction, but also new technologies will be crucial to limiting the devastating effects of climate change globally. Not only is innovation needed to combat these issues more than ever, but also new methods of promoting and adopting well-acknowledged methods of prevention such as mass reforestation, and carbon capture and storage.

Pandemics

We didn't originally have this section included (ironic given that Quinn received his degree in immunology and global health), but just before submitting this final manuscript, Covid-19 struck. As you surely know, the world is a different place because of it. The increasing interconnectedness of our world and the resulting dependencies that this connectedness produces mean pandemics are both more likely and exponentially more drastic in their effect (we certainly hope you're reading this by lamplight, and not some flickering candle amidst the rubble of a post-Covid apocalyptic hellscape). Without going too much further, preventing future pandemics will be a massive challenge and opportunity for new startups (see BlueDot, the Canadian company that first spotted Covid-19).

The power of youth

Youth have, since time immemorial, received the short end of the stick. Older generations have always lamented the irresponsibility of the next generation. Even in the age of the ancient Greeks, the old complained about the new. In his Book III of *Odes,* in around 20 BC, the Roman poet Horace wrote 'our sires' age was worse than our grandsires'. We, their sons, are more worthless than they; so in our turn we shall give the world a progeny yet more corrupt'.[7] That's really flowery language for 'the reason millennials can't afford homes is because they're eating too much avocado toast.' But that's not all your youth stands to offer you; from personal experience, youth has always been a double-edged sword, and when wielded correctly, you can just about always make it work for you.

Underestimation or advantage?

Generally speaking, older generations perpetually underestimate the skill and ability of youth, which happens to be potentially advantageous for you. First, doing something, anything at all, becomes more impressive when you do it while you're young. The more you do, the more impressive! You have the ability to leverage your accomplishments for far more than they're worth because of your age. This means you don't have to start so big – start something, anything, even if it's a club at your school. Take on positions of leadership where you can, develop a resume of leadership, and these things will provide you with access to the people and places you need later on to help your business grow quickly and be successful. Second, today's youth are more connected and culturally competent than any generation previously thanks to the wonders of smartphones, the internet, and all the other incredible technological innovations of the past decade. The knowledge that comes with that connectivity is incredibly powerful. Use it.

Notes

1 Chakrabarti, R (2017) 9 out of 10 start-ups fail. Here's why! *Entrepreneur*, www.entrepreneur.com/article/295798 (archived at https://perma.cc/X6P3-62AS)

2 WHO (2021) Climate change and health, http://www.who.int/news-room/fact-sheets/detail/climate-change-and-health (archived at https://perma.cc/HTP8-DGAW)

3 Stern, N (2014) Summary of Conclusions, in *The Economics of Climate Change*, xv–xx, http://doi.org/10.1017/cbo978051181 7434.003 (archived at https://perma.cc/2SXF-PPCG)

4 Zimmerman, K (2017) 5 things we know millennials want from a job, *Forbes*, https://www.forbes.com/sites/kaytiezimmerman/2017/10/01/5-things-we-know-millennials-want-from-a-job/#5f0f9f7c7809 (archived at https://perma.cc/R7CK-B9WV)

5 Stern (2014)

6 The Bulletin (nd) Doomsday Clock, https://thebulletin.org/doomsday-clock/ (archived at https://perma.cc/LFT4-W3UG)

7 Sedar, J (2013) 15 historical complaints about young people ruining everything, *Mental Floss*, http://mentalfloss.com/article/52209/15-historical-complaints-about-young-people-ruining-everything (archived at https://perma.cc/CGA9-7ZZH)

02
Misconceptions when starting a company

When the term 'entrepreneur' is mentioned, what's the first association that forms in your mind? Perhaps it's a person wearing expensive formal wear, emerging from their excessively large private jet. Maybe instead you envision a boardroom full of executives, sitting in silence as the CEO leads a meeting about company-wide sales reaching a record high in the past year. It seems that in this day and age, entrepreneurship has become more popularized than ever before. The downside of this fascination is it carries with it many misconceptions around starting a company. There are four main ones we've noticed, and we would like to dispel them for you right now: that entrepreneurship is glamorous by practice; it's filled with people; it can make you a quick buck; and entrepreneurs are *born* with a natural ability to build a company.

'Entrepreneurship is glamorous'

There's a false perception of entrepreneurs enjoying extravagant lifestyles topped with foreign cars and massive estates.

All it takes is a short scroll through Instagram to see these self-proclaimed 'entrepreneurs' flaunt their wealth and portray starting a business as a stress-free, relatively simple way to possess material goods. As the saying goes, if something seems too good to be true, it probably is. What social media ultimately shows is the end result of entrepreneurship (for some), the inkling of success that is unearthed after countless hours dedicated to the craft. What fails to make the picture or video clip on social media, what does not reap as many likes but is fundamental to the glory, is the time that is spent working with your head down as an entrepreneur. Particularly, it's the innate belief that the grind that you're putting yourself through, the time and energy you're contributing to building your company without any guarantee of return, is going to be worth it when all is said and done. This requires an unparalleled level of mental toughness and perseverance that not everyone has, or is willing to subject themselves to. The glamour that is demonstrated by the media is far from the reality of entrepreneurship on a daily basis. The truth is, about 80 per cent of the day-to-day work done by an entrepreneur is not what is typically deemed to be desirable. These necessary miscellaneous tasks include going through legal agreements, checking and responding to emails, commuting to different destinations, scheduling appointments etc. What drives entrepreneurs to complete these mundane and sometimes tedious tasks is their genuine desire and hunger for the overall process. Effective entrepreneurs hold the mindset that each mundane task will help move the needle for their business in some way, and this idea alone is enough to drive their motivation to accomplish these activities, day in and day out. Early on in the life of your company, you will often find yourself occupied with the ongoing responsibility of putting out fires as they appear, or handling any unexpected problems that arise from the ordinary operation of your business. This is what the regular day in the life of an entrepreneur looks like, which is quite contrary to the false yet attractive depiction that is increasingly becoming normalized by social media.

'Entrepreneurship is filled with people'

Another common misconception that is typically associated with entrepreneurship is that it's a process that consists of many people involved from start to finish. There is the tendency to picture entrepreneurs constantly with a large team around them working to navigate through this shared goal, or to envision entrepreneurs spending a large portion of their day with clients. The reality is that, especially in your first year building your company, the journey of entrepreneurship is very lonely. Early on, you often spend the majority of your day working alone on your idea, trying to figure out how you can turn your mental vision into a viable business that people can understand and engage with. Given how much work is done in isolation with your idea, you may also find that you forgo time spent with your friends and family. There is a healthy balance (which is different for everyone) that you must strike to ensure that you're keeping your happiness and mental well-being a priority while you build your company. It's pivotal to your success that you create an effective schedule for yourself, whether that be in a physical agenda or in Google Calendar, where you input not only your work responsibilities (meetings, product demos etc) but also the time you're setting aside to spend with your loved ones. If you don't add it to your calendar, you're not going to give this downtime its due importance.

Another way to alleviate some of the loneliness that you experience as an entrepreneur is to actively try to find a community of fellow entrepreneurs to connect with. From Swish's experience, he found this sense of community by joining a recreational basketball league with a few of his friends and fellow founders. Having this community of other entrepreneurs by your side can provide all parties involved with a sense of consolation, that you're not the only one undergoing this journey of entrepreneurship and there are other individuals around you who are experiencing the same anxieties. Where exactly can you find this kind of community? The easiest and often most effective way is through social media platforms like LinkedIn, Facebook and Instagram. All it takes is a straightforward direct message asking other founders if they would be interested in spending an hour each week doing something that you mutually enjoy, no matter the activity. The important thing is that you have that regular social event or hobby to look forward to each week and that you're putting yourself out there for others to connect with.

In addition, a recommended tactic to relieve some of the stress and pressure felt from daily activities as a founder is to practice meditation techniques. The most notable figures around the world credit daily meditation for their high performance because it helps them to maintain their mental toughness. When it comes to meditation, LeBron James has said, '(mental fitness) is something I've always prioritized, and it's just as important to my game, and my life, as anything I can do physically'.[1] Apps like Headspace or Calm can be used to simplify meditation, and you can engage in a session for any preferred length of time. With the difficulties of entrepreneurship, it must be restated: if you're ever feeling down in the process of building your company, understand that this is completely normal and you're not alone in this feeling. Every founder has at some point felt discouraged or anxious when striving for their goal, which comes with the territory in a risk-bearing career like entrepreneurship. Strides have been made in recent years to break the stigma around mental health and entrepreneurship, but continuing the conversation is still worthwhile. In these moments, remember what you're fighting for and lean on your community of fellow entrepreneurs who have had or are currently facing similar experiences.

'Entrepreneurship can make you a quick buck'

The next misconception about entrepreneurship that should be dispelled is that building a company can help you make a quick buck. It's understandable why many people have this train of thought; it seems that there is a new company being sold for millions of dollars every day. We have become accustomed to the belief that by simply thinking of a new business idea and incorporating it, we can become the next Mark Zuckerberg in a year's time. That is just not the reality of entrepreneurship and the numbers prove it. You may have heard the common statistic that nine out of every ten startups fail;[2] this is not entirely accurate. According to the Small Business Association, these failure figures are as follows: 30 per cent of new businesses fail (go bankrupt) within the first two years of launching, 50 per cent fail during the first five years, and 66 per cent fail during the first 10 years.[3] You might be thinking that these figures are not as daunting as you had imagined. What you need to consider is that starting your business will involve capital investment that only escalates as you begin to scale and expand. Expenditures that aren't properly fore-casted arise every so often and before you know it, you can quickly wind up in a situation where you're in a deep finan-cial deficit. Borrowing money from the bank can only take you so far, and if you're not careful (specifically if your busi-ness is a sole proprietorship) your lenders will also have the right to your personal assets. Simply put, there are much faster ways to make money than entrepreneurship.

It's absolutely imperative that you don't start your com-pany with the intention of selling it off as soon as possible. If you become an entrepreneur for this 'get rich quick' purpose, you're in for a huge disappointment and will almost certainly be miserable when things don't go as planned. When Surf was in its development stages, the company faced several obstacles that stood in the way of its progression. Legal issues such as trademark violations, in addition to product delays, were some of the hurdles that the company encountered. To the entrepreneur who is only in the game for the sake of sell-ing their company as quickly as they can, these hindrances will act as reasons to quit immediately. What kept co-founders Swish and Aanikh motivated to work through these hardships was their genuine appreciation for the gradual process that is entrepreneurship.

True respect and admiration for entrepreneurship comes from thinking through your intentions for building your business before you embark on the journey. Who are you trying to help? What change are you trying to make to the existing way of doing things? How will you make an impact and what will the legacy of your company be? Answering these questions will cement a clear purpose for your work and will provide you with an inkling of ambition when you're stuck in those moments contemplating whether entrepreneurship is worth it or not. As (Canadian) comedian Jim Carrey once said in a commencement speech, 'The effect you have on others is the most valuable currency there is'.[4] Internalizing this quote as a mindset for evaluating success will push you past adversity in a way that endlessly chasing money will not.

'Entrepreneurs are born'

Jan Koum was born and raised in a small village in Kiev, Ukraine. His father worked as a construction worker and his mother a housewife. The family of three lived in a small house without hot water. At 16, Jan and his mother emigrated to California amid the tumultuous sociopolitical climate in their homeland. They lived in a measly two-bedroom apartment (through government aid) and Jan could often be found lining up for food stamps to put food on the family's table.[5] Calamity struck shortly afterwards when his mother was diagnosed with cancer, and the family had to get by on disability allowance cheques. On the academic side, Jan was not a great student and was considered a troublemaker by his schoolteachers. He did, however, pick up one skill in his teen years. Jan taught himself computer programming by the age of 18, by buying used instructional guides from a bookstore and returning them when he completed his study. His expertise in computer networking was enough for him to land a job as an infrastructure engineer at Yahoo! while he was still an undergraduate. He spent nine years working for the company, until he recognized the fascinating rise in popularity of digital apps. In 2009, Jan incorporated WhatsApp Inc., which in 2014 was bought by Facebook in a $19 billion deal.[6] Koum, like many other founders, is an example of an entrepreneur who did not have any aspirations for starting his own company for a large portion of his life; Koum was likely more concerned about where his family's next meal would come from than building a company. Contrary to how things are now, entrepreneurship was not always perceived as a viable career option to pursue.

There was a time when entrepreneurship was only considered to be a career for people who were otherwise unemployed.[7] An evident stigma surrounded the term, and when someone would call themselves an entrepreneur, it meant they were either extremely wealthy (they could therefore take on such financial risk easily) or they couldn't find a job and so they decided to start their own business instead. Entrepreneurship has become a valuable asset to the global economy, with entrepreneurs actually being encouraged to spur innovation and compete against other firms internationally. For instance, the Ontario provincial government in Canada currently provides entrepreneurship grants and resources to citizens aged 15 to 29, including a 'summer company' initiative in which successful applicants are provided with up to $1,500 upfront to help with start-up costs. Government-funded programmes for entrepreneurs were completely unheard of when our parents were our age; this is a true testament to how far entrepreneurship has come in its public acceptance.

Given the development of entrepreneurship as a career, what makes an individual want to become an entrepreneur? According to a 2016 Amway Global Entrepreneurship Report, the two motivating factors for those who decide to pursue entrepreneurship as a career are the need for independence from an employer, and the pursuit of self-fulfilment.[8] Yet beyond these two general drivers, there are certain things common to all genuine entrepreneurs (in contrast to self-proclaimed ones) that make them who they are. It must be acknowledged that none of these similarities are in any way related to intellect, which you're born with, hence all of these abilities can be developed no matter who you are. Sure, to some capacity it's beneficial to have natural intellect and be able to learn quickly. This can only take you so far, however, especially in the marathon that is entrepreneurship, where everyone generally starts their company from zero and builds their way up.

People who have the entrepreneurial spirit share a mutual focus toward the *execution* of their ideas. There is a belief that a great idea, if not executed upon, will remain just that: an idea. These individuals don't settle on mental propositions, but instead make it their mission to put their vision into action. As Thomas Edison put it bluntly, 'vision without execution is just hallucination'. Adequate execution involves exposing your product to the market, gathering information, and iterating different forms of an idea, as opposed to sitting back and waiting for someone else to make your mind's creation a reality. Another quality that all entrepreneurs have in common is their relentless persistence, continuing to chip away at problems until they find solutions. They don't let obstacles deter them for a substantial amount of time.

Entrepreneurs recognize that hardships and failures are a part of the process, and the ultimate destination cannot be arrived at without these bumps in the road. How do they actively develop perseverance, especially when they haven't yet fought through adversity in their lives? Real perseverance is fostered through facing ambiguity and unfamiliar situations head-on. Put yourself in circumstances that make your stomach turn. Set goals for yourself that you initially feel are out of your capability to accomplish. Create actionable steps to gradually move the needle on these goals. Enlist the help of a friend who is also attempting to achieve a specific goal. Hold each other accountable on a regular basis for the decisions you make that are either advancing or receding your progress toward your respective goals. Perseverance is the by-product of willingly doing something that makes you uncomfortable, over and over again. It's by subjecting yourself to something you don't want to do, in hopes of accomplishing some desirable end result, that you can develop unparalleled focus.

It can be argued that these entrepreneurial traits can be developed by alternative means outside of entrepreneurship. A response to this is advice that Swish has received from his long-time mentor Manny Padda, Founder, New Avenue Capital. Manny often says, 'Everyone can develop entrepreneurial tendencies but to have the heart and spirit of an entrepreneur comes only by taking a leap of faith and immersing yourself in your project.' This advice echoes the sentiment that many founders share, that entrepreneurship cannot be taught. Rather, it's something that must be learned through first-hand experience, which includes making mistakes and building from them, facing setbacks and overcoming them, testing what works and enhancing it gradually. Perhaps Reid Hoffman, co-founder and former executive chairman of LinkedIn, described entrepreneurship best when he remarked, 'An entrepreneur is someone who will jump off a cliff and assemble an airplane on the way down'.[9] This is the level of ambiguity (and near insanity) involved in becoming an entrepreneur. It's not a career that you're born with the instinct of pursuing; instead it's the cumulation of personal experiences and developed personality traits that compel an individual to take the risk of starting their own business.

Notes

1 Gagne, Y (2019) LeBron James partners with Calm to improve your mental fitness, *Fast Company*, https://www.fastcompany.com/90441135/lebron-james-partners-with-calm-to-improve-your-mental-fitness (archived at https://perma.cc/C7CT-874H)

2 Chakrabarti, R (2017) 9 out of 10 start-ups fail. Here's why! *Entrepreneur*, www.entrepreneur.com/article/295798 (archived at https://perma.cc/F2PR-GFVB)

3 McIntyre, G (2020) What percentage of small businesses fail? *Fundera*, https://www.fundera.com/blog/what-percentage-of-small-businesses-fail (archived at https://perma.cc/KKG4-A6Y9)

4 Maharishi International University (2014) Full speech: Jim Carrey's commencement address at the 2014 MUM graduation (EN, FR, ES, RU, GR,...), *YouTube*, www.youtube.com/watch?v=V80-gPkpH6M (archived at https://perma.cc/5C4X-MDG4)

5 Olson, P (2014) Exclusive: The rags-to-riches tale of how Jan Koum built WhatsApp into Facebook's new $19 billion baby, *Forbes*, https://www.forbes.com/sites/parmyolson/2014/02/19/exclusive-inside-story-how-jan-koum-built-whatsapp-into-facebooks-new-19-billion-baby/#5d047d782fa1 (archived at https://perma.cc/G7W8-35C7)

6 Ibid

7 Reich, R (2010) Opinion | Entrepreneur or Unemployed? *New York Times*, www.nytimes.com/2010/06/02/opinion/02reich. html. (archived at https://perma.cc/LL7P-SQR2)

8 Amway (2016) Amway Global Entrepreneurship Report reveals American attitudes and confidence in self-employment rise above the global average, *Multivu*, http://www.multivu.com/ players/English/7784253-2016-amway-global-entrepreneurship-report/ (archived at https://perma.cc/H4DV-6RYB)

9 Taylor, C (2018) LinkedIn co-founder Reid Hoffman says starting a company is like 'jumping off a cliff', *CNBC*, www. cnbc.com/2018/11/02/linkedin-co-founder-reid-hoffman-says-starting-a-company-is-like-jumping-off-a-cliff.html (archived at https://perma.cc/V47P-8ZP3)

Part Two
Endeavour

03
Getting started

Traditionally, starting a business followed a well-travelled path: develop a concept, develop a product, test the product, launch the product. This is called the Product Development Model, which we would suggest is *not* how you should approach building a business. This model is dependent on the classical thinking: 'Build it and they will come.' That's exactly what *doesn't* happen in today's world. Part of the reason so many startups fail is because people focus on building a great piece of technology or a great service, and they forget that building an incredible product doesn't necessarily guarantee that people are going to buy it. We live in a world where 90 per cent of the data on the internet has been created since 2016, as per a 2019 study;[1] the rate at which new information is created and introduced is quite literally unimaginable. In an age of total information saturation, building a business with the hope that people will discover your product or service by happenstance just doesn't make sense.

Step one: start with the problem

The issue with the Product Development Model is it revolves around a great product, not a great *problem*. People don't buy or use products that don't solve their problems, and are reluctant to purchase anything they don't *think* will. Building a great product or service is a fundamental part of any successful business, but it shouldn't be where you start: don't start with the idea, start with the problem. Build for people and the problems they have – not the problems you tell *them* they have, but rather the problems they tell *you* they have. Ultimately, apart from poor team chemistry, the number one reason for a company's failure is a lack of customers purchasing their solution. Why? Because whatever the solution is, if it isn't addressing a problem that customers will pay for, it cannot become profitable.

Building your business around a customer problem also means building your business around a customer solution, working with customers to understand what they want and how they want it. Some of the world's largest companies espouse this perspective and run on a strongly customer-centric business model – Amazon is one famous example.

What is the process of getting started? We'll give it a flashy and exciting name like the 'customer development model' (we didn't come up with that, it's a broadly recognized best practice): identify a customer problem, identify a potential solution to that problem, validate that hypothetical solution through user feedback, and once you've achieved customer validation, move on to actually building your solution! Throughout this process you must constantly consult with potential customers to better understand how to best meet their needs, even after customer validation. So, let's get started.

The problem

First things first, identify a potential problem. Starting with the right problem is crucial to ensuring the future success of your business: the bigger the problem, the better. It's important to note that flexibility is key – as you begin the process of investigating different issues in different markets, you'll learn more about what people or businesses really need fixed, and your selected problem will likely change or evolve. If it doesn't you're either extremely lucky, a genius, or deceiving yourself.

So how should you select your problem? The sky's the limit; the world is full of problems, pick one. A simple but effective method is to begin by outlining the characteristics of what an 'ideal' problem for you to address might look like. The following are a number of general guidelines or problem characteristics that should help to narrow down your search. We would argue that aiming big is only a good thing, but for those interested in doing something on a more local scale, the following characteristics are relevant but should be taken more generally, ie the problem might not be a billion-dollar one, but it is sufficiently large enough that people would willingly pay for a solution!

Global problems

The problem should be global in scale. For every venture you start, there is a significant opportunity cost – the opportunities you pass up in order to pursue your venture are undoubtedly significant, and it's critical to ensure that your venture is worthwhile in the first place. This is particularly true for those in school; summer internships or potential career opportunities are numerous, and your opportunity cost will be high. This isn't necessarily a bad thing, it simply means you're more likely to pursue a venture if it's truly worthwhile, which is how it should be.

Painful problems

The problem should be painful. Ask yourself, is it the kind of problem that people or businesses recognize and care about? Will they care enough to pay for your solution? The more people care, the more they will pay. Too many businesses, especially in the tech industry, try to solve problems that people just don't care that much about. This is particularly true of apps. The colloquialism 'there's an app for that' exists for a reason; with more than six million apps between Google Play and Apple's App Store alone there are a whole lot of apps that solve virtually no problem whatsoever.[2] Take the chat app 'Yo' as an example. It does nothing more than allow you to message the word 'Yo' to friends. That's all. It took eight hours to code and raised $1 million in seed funding. However urgently one may need to send a friend a 'Yo', it just isn't the sort of thing any customer will pay for – that the founder was able to secure a million in seed funding is a testament to his genius, the VC's stupidity, or something else fully undecipherable. We would also make the case that there are many more pressing issues that you should spend your time working to solve.

The following characteristics are for entrepreneurs that are looking to build massive startups that alter the fabric of our society. This is really hard to do (neither Quinn nor Swish have done it... yet) but it's worth exploring and understanding how you would approach building a company of that scale.

Billion-dollar problems

The problem should have a market size of more than $1 billion. In other words, if everyone in the world that experienced your particular problem were to purchase your solution, would that total revenue amount to more than $1 billion? When you go to investors, you will need to present a case for why your particular solution is worth investing in. One of the primary ways you would do this is by outlining the total addressable market (TAM) of your solution, in the case that if you receive the investor's money, you will be able to 'capture' a larger portion of that total addressable market. Investors evaluate how much of that market you're likely to capture based on how much you've already captured, how large the market is, how many competitors offer similar solutions, etc. The idea is, the bigger the market, the larger your potential value as a company. As a rule of thumb, companies that focus on problems with a market size below $1 billion tend to draw much less investment.

Outsized returns

The problem should provide a potential return on investment for investors of at least 10X. For many investors, this characteristic acts as a threshold for determining whether your company is worth considering for investment. The question then becomes, how do investors determine if your solution has the potential to generate 10X returns on their investment? Every investor has a slightly different method of calculating this, including everything from team composition to market size. The most common and basic method involves calculating the portion of the market you will *realistically* generate revenue from as a proportion of the market you could *potentially* generate revenue from if you were to grow substantially.

Calculating 10X returns

Calculating the portion of the market you will *realistically* generate revenue from as a proportion of the market you could *potentially* generate revenue from if you were to grow substantially can be understood by calculating your Total Addressable Market (TAM), Serviceable Addressable Market (SAM), and Serviceable Obtainable Market (SOM).[3] This section explains what these are and how to calculate them, which is an important first step towards justifying the assumptions you'll make about your company's future potential.

The Total Addressable Market (TAM) is the total market size if every person who experienced the problem you're solving paid you for your solution. The TAM is generally enormous and more of a conceptual ceiling than anything else – but it helps you understand how large your company could become. Serviceable Addressable Market (SAM) is the potential market if your company grows well and is able to provide a solution that many customers in your segment want and are willing to pay for. The Serviceable Obtainable Market (SOM) is the amount of annual revenue you will reasonably capture within two to four years, if not already.

Talking to customers about your problem

If there is one thing you should spend the most time on when getting started with your company, it is talking to users. There is nothing that will teach you more or do more to further the progress of your company than talking to users and better understanding their problems. Talking to users is such an important part of the startup process that there have been entire books dedicated to it alone – our favourite is *The Mom Test: How to talk to customers and learn if your business is a good idea when everyone is lying to you* by Rob Fitzpatrick.[4]

So how should you go about talking to potential customers? Three key takeaways to keep in mind are:

- *'Talk about their life instead of your idea.'*
  People you speak with will want to support you, because more often than not, people are nice. This is really problematic when you're looking for an unbiased indicator of whether or not what you're working on is a good idea. Asking them about their life (and in particular the problem they bring up, whether or not it's the problem you had planned on focusing on) is a great way to do that. Don't talk about your idea.

- *'Ask about specifics in the past instead of generics or opinions about the future.'*
  When you're talking to users, the key thing to keep in mind is that you don't want to get their opinion, you want to understand their actual behaviour. Opinions are worthless – everyone says, 'I might use that' or 'yeah, that would be valuable'. But unless their actual behaviour indicates that that's the case, it can't be trusted. Because if your problem isn't painful enough that they're already trying to solve it, it's not a big enough problem.

- *'Talk less and listen more.'*
  This one is pretty self-explanatory. Don't pitch, listen.

The challenge is to collect authentic insights when everyone around you (ie your mom) is trying to be supportive and likely not providing you with an authentic depiction of how they actually view your product; and it makes sense that the first people you talk to probably want to help you, and be as supportive as they can. The bias those sentiments introduce can be fatal, propelling you forward with a fuel of false positives.

Moreover, the more invested you are in your idea, the more likely you are to spend time pitching to users rather than understanding their problems. As a result, many founders receive false confirmation that what they are building is valuable and end up spending a lot of time and energy on the wrong thing – this is really painful to go through. Remember, user *research* (that's what this is) is a dramatically different process than user *testing*; in user *testing* you actually put your product in front of users and have them narrate their thoughts or feelings as they navigate it (more on this later).

Substantial improvement (solution)

While you may still be focused on identifying a problem to tackle, we've included this section and the following for those of you with the beginnings of a solution in mind. The reason it's included here is that this is an iterative process; after identifying a potential problem you will identify potential customers, and then begin to develop a fuller solution, and then verify your solution and market focus by repeating this entire process to ensure you're building to the needs of your customers. Your solution must be a substantial improvement to existing products or services that address the same problem. The general rule is that in order to have people switch from existing solutions, yours needs to be an order of magnitude better.

Global problems, local solutions (solution)

One of the things many people do, particularly youth, is focus on problems that are immediately relevant to them. This will frequently lead people to develop solutions that are limited in scope and focused only on the local manifestation of the problem. This isn't a bad thing and can rather be incredibly beneficial – limiting scope and focusing means you're more likely to build something people love. The key is to be aware of that limited scope, and actively consider how your solution might scale to address a global manifestation of your problem. Thinking on a global scale is difficult for many, particularly students and youth for whom expectations are generally lower, and for whom experience is generally limited – our hope is that this book helps you begin to think on a global scale. Be audacious in your expectations for yourself and your company.

An example of this would be university students building a startup focused on eliminating food waste across events hosted on campus. That's exactly what Swish and Quinn set out to do in their first year at the University of Toronto together; we called the company Foogo. We started by focusing only on events and small on-campus restaurants. As we began talking with small stores, we realized this was a problem felt by local grocers, farms, massive multinational grocery chains and almost every stakeholder along the supply chain from food production to distribution to consumption. There was a global problem behind the local issue we had first identified.

Step two: refining your problem

B2B versus B2C

When identifying a potential problem, you'll be looking at the problems experienced by either individuals or businesses. Which one you address will dictate your business model: Business to Business (B2B) or Business to Consumer (B2C). The former includes any business that sells its goods or services predominantly to other businesses, eg sales management software, cloud storage, etc. The latter comprises businesses that sell to individual consumers, and includes household names such as Apple, Nike, Louis Vuitton, etc. Both B2B and B2C business models have advantages and disadvantages; understanding them will better position you to decide how you want to focus your business.

Business to Business

We'll begin by describing B2B and B2C businesses more fully before breaking down the major pros and cons of each. The major driving factors behind a B2B business are the relationships they have with their customers, product features, and the quality of customer support. The primary motivation for purchase by customers is to establish a competitive or strategic advantage, or to generate value. Product complexity is generally higher for B2B businesses as the number of features for a given product is much higher, and subsequently product pricing is generally both higher and more customized to the needs of the customer. Market size is usually much more focused and niche. For B2B businesses, sales and marketing is focused on building a relationship with the customer as the sales process takes longer and the business-customer relationship lasts longer.

Business to Consumer

The major driving factors behind a B2C business's success are product features and brand appeal. The primary motivations for purchase by customers have to do with status, personal gratification, emotional attachment, need, affordability and utility. Product complexity is generally lesser for B2C businesses, accompanied by comparatively lower pricing. Market size is much larger, and sales and marketing is focused on maximizing transaction value as the business-customer relationship, and subsequently the sales process, is much shorter.

B2C businesses are more dynamic, selling to fickle target customers with continually evolving preferences. The dynamism of B2C customers drives new technology development and generally means business is faster paced. While customers are more fickle, the market for B2C products is generally much larger, though the potential revenue per consumer is much lower. Sales and marketing focuses much more on the values and emotional state of individual consumers and is consequently of much greater importance to B2C businesses than B2B ones.

It is important to note that a company need not be B2B or B2C; there are a variety of ways by which to combine aspects of both. For example, most companies selling consumer packaged goods – products that are sold quickly and at relatively low cost – such as L'Oréal or Pepsi, employ a B2B2C business model, wherein their products are generally sold to other businesses who are then responsible for reselling to individual consumers. Companies such as Amazon employ other models such as C2C, in which consumers sell directly to consumers through Amazon's platform. The point here is there is no one method by which to build your company but understanding the basic characteristics of the most common models, B2B and B2C, will allow you to better select your initial target market or customer segment.

Market segmentation

After you've identified a general problem to focus on, it is useful to do what is called market segmentation. Doing this allows you to begin better understanding the customers afflicted by the particular problem you've focused on, and sets the groundwork for your business model, customer profile, and a variety of other documents that you will need to establish your business, apply for grants, incubators and accelerators, and raise funding.

If you're a B2C business, you're only really interested in the granularity of segmentation – partitioning customers based on geography, demography, psychographic factors, or consumer behaviour. Market segmentation for B2B businesses entails identifying a specific economic sector to be broken down into a collection of industries, with each industry comprising several market segments. Every nation's economy comprises multiple sectors which broadly categorize nearly all of the business activity in that nation's economy. The US economy, for example, is broken down into the following sectors: mining; finance and insurance; real estate, rental and leasing; manufacturing; wholesale trade; retail trade; transportation; information; management of companies and enterprises; utilities; construction; administrative; support; waste management and remediation services; educational services; health care and social assistance; arts; entertainment and recreation; accommodation and food services; other services (except public administration); professional; and scientific and technical services.[5] Other countries will have varying economic sectors when compared to this list – most countries probably won't have quite as many.

Industry segmentation

After choosing a sector to begin investigating, you'll need to select a specific industry to narrow down further; each industry is made up of a collection of market segments. A market segment is a category of customers who have similar preferences. For example, if you were to choose the information sector, you'd find the industries of telecommunications, publishing and data processing, among others.

Once you've selected an industry, it then becomes a matter of choosing how you will segment it. How you segment your industry partially depends on the particular problem you're investigating and on your solution to that problem.

Step three: customer personas

In the previous section, you broke down various market segments to better understand who your potential customers might be and the major problems they face. This next section is devoted to developing customer personas, archetypes you construct of your ideal customer to better understand their needs and how you can meet them. This step is crucial to narrowing down your customer segment further and iterating on your segment focus based on real feedback from real customers. In other words, you want to be able to verify the customer personas you build with your target customers in real life. This can be done in a variety of ways: reading blogs or websites; watching videos in which industry professionals discuss answers to the questions below; setting up coffee chats or calls to discuss these questions with industry professionals; emailing or messaging industry professionals on LinkedIn with one or two of these questions; meeting with academics who study your chosen industry to hear their perspective on the needs of your target customer segment. However you go about it, if you're planning on building a B2B business, make sure you collect the opinions of multiple stakeholders in different positions in different companies; and if you're planning on building a B2C business, talk directly with consumers you think would most want to purchase your product or service.

Before contacting members of your target segment, go through the following questions and write your answers in bullet form:

1 Where do your customers live on the internet? (This will be crucial in understanding what platforms to reach them on and how to reach out to them.)

2 Do your customers currently use any products or services that help them solve the problem you are looking to address?

3 What signals to you that this is an urgent problem for your customers?

These are the assumptions you're making about your customer, but going on assumptions alone isn't a great way to start a company – that's why you need to contact target customers directly. Aim for one to two meetings a week until you're able to verify these assumptions using what you've learned. Realistically this process will never end, and every time you meet with potential customers you should be working to better understand their needs and adapting your solution to better meet them. Here, we recommend you get at least five separate sources before moving on to subsequent sections, but that number should never stop growing.

The lightbulb moment

Usually in books like this, the section on 'Lightbulb' moments comes *before* the one on 'Getting Started'. It seems intuitive – getting started on an idea without an idea sounds like a pretty unreasonable thing to do. As it turns out, going about starting a business that way is responsible for approximately 48 per cent of all startup failures.[6] We're here to tell you that the real lightbulb moment should only come *after* you've identified a problem faced by your potential customers. In fact, it's not so much of a lightbulb moment as a combination of your own ingenuity and a careful analysis of your customers' needs. It is likely, however, that most of you reading this book are doing so because you have an idea and want to know how to build a business on the basis of that idea. This is not a bad thing; starting with an idea does not ensure future failure. What *will* ensure failure is an unwillingness to change or modify your solution based on your research and interactions with your customers. Indeed, as we have outlined, you must first select an industry segment to evaluate before moving further. Having an idea as to how you might solve a particular problem can serve as a welcome starting point for narrowing down your industry focus – so long as you allow your research to mould your solution, not vice versa.

Before we start, we're going to go over a couple of misconceptions when it comes to lightbulb moments, creativity and innovation. It is possible to increase your chances of having a lightbulb idea; entire lives have been devoted to understanding the psychology of creativity and how to promote it. The general consensus is that there are two phases to creative imagination. The first is 'divergent thinking', or the ability to think of a wide variety of ideas, all of which have some connection to a central problem or topic.[7] Divergent thinking tends to be driven by intuitive thinking, which is fast and automatic. The second phase is 'convergent thinking', which is used to evaluate the ideas generated through divergent thinking for usefulness within the context of the central topic or problem. Convergent thinking is driven by more conscious and analytical thinking, which is slow and deliberate, facilitating the selection of the *right* idea. Research demonstrates that selecting the right idea from many is improved through exposure and experience. The more experience you have in a field, the better able you are to select from amongst your intuitively generated ideas. This seems rather intuitive – if you have experience in a particular field, you're less likely to select fallible ideas.[8]

What is perhaps more interesting, and useful in the context of this chapter, is research demonstrating that more novel ideas come from connecting two otherwise disparate concepts.[9] Society has often associated genius with the apparent 'unintuitiveness' of an individual's idea. Alternatively, genius is the ability to connect two or more concepts that few else would have thought to connect. This is a fallible narrative – research demonstrates that no one mind is intuitively more or less able to cross conceptual gaps between two or more concepts. Instead, the ability to identify or create connections between two or more concepts is dependent on how close the mind perceives those two concepts to be. That degree of closeness is dependent on the unique wiring of the brain and how it has associated those two concepts in the past. Hence, what seems to be a stroke of genius to some is in fact a rather intuitive leap for others with different experiences, perspectives and upbringings.

Cultivate curiosity

This notion of creativity that depends more on the diversity of experience and perception provides us with useful insights. It tells us that constant inquiry, the cultivation of diverse experiences and the entertainment of diverse perspectives facilitates conceptual connections that would be otherwise unavailable. In simpler terms, the more diverse your experiences, intellectual or otherwise, the more able you are to arrive at conclusions others may not be able to so easily. Earlier in the book, it was claimed that 'when you start asking the questions no one else is asking, you start getting answers no one else has'. The research outlined here provides further evidence of this claim. Hence, our first recommendation on this topic of creativity is in fact the same made previously – cultivate an endless curiosity. Ask why, repeatedly.

Look for problems

The second practice that we've found works particularly well is as follows: in every interaction you have with someone who works in a different discipline, studies a different field, or is in any way remarkably different from yourself, ask them what their problems are. Ask what kind of day-to-day pains they face in their work, their leisure, or at any other time. As an entrepreneur you're in the business of solving problems, and you're not ever going to be able to think of or know them all (this is a good thing). With each new issue you identify, you're presented with an opportunity to innovate. To call upon your unique perspective and leverage it to lessen the pains of another.

There are three major benefits to this practice: first, it provides you with a unique method for distinguishing yourself as someone with an authentic interest in the concerns and problems of others; second, it provides you with a better understanding of what kind of problems people feel most readily – selection bias ensures that you only hear about the problems that affect people the most; and third, psychologically it promotes authenticity and vulnerability, key to establishing longer and more mutually beneficial relationships.

If there's one thing you take away from what we are trying to say here, it's be curious and stay that way.

Reflect

One of the first things you learn as an entrepreneur is that there are always too many things competing for your time. The key is identifying those tasks that are most important and actually contribute to moving things forward: taking the time to reflect is one of them. Almost all of the breakthroughs Quinn has had while working on Autumn, Arzela, or any of the other companies he started or contributed to, came when he put time aside for himself to sit and reflect on everything that was happening around me. Designating time, explicitly putting it in your calendar, and taking 15 to 20 minutes every day to sit, think, and write your thoughts down is the single most valuable habit either of us have formed over the course of our careers so far.

All of humanity's problems stem from man's inability to sit quietly in a room alone.

BLAISE PASCAL

Read

Second only to reflection, reading is one of the single most important things you can do outside of running your company. As an entrepreneur, you are tasked with constantly reevaluating what you believe and why you believe it; each assumption you make has to be critically evaluated and tested, and more often than not you're being told you're wrong by those around you. Reading opens your mind to an incredible array of perspectives, builds your empathy, inspires creativity, and expands your critical thinking skills. Whether you read fiction or nonfiction, the vast knowledge to be gained will make you a far superior entrepreneur and, frankly, human being. As a rule, Quinn tries to read at least one book a month on a topic or area of knowledge in which he is completely ignorant; and more often than not, that information has become useful, if not critical, to the way he runs his company. There is a reason every popular leader, academic, or entrepreneur reads as much as they do – because not doing so would mean limiting the information they have to make the critical decisions they make each day.

Non-consensus beliefs

When it comes to developing a solution, one of the first things you must ask yourself is why your proposed solution hasn't already been made. Presumably, if the problem you're looking to solve is a painful one and the global market size is massive, there has to be some reason others haven't previously thought of and implemented something similar.

There will always be those that are better capitalized (have more money), smarter, more experienced, more connected, etc. Competing with giants such as Facebook, Google, Microsoft and Apple is incredibly difficult, and being successful means having some insight or belief about the world that they don't share. Because if they did, they would build and launch what you're hoping to build but far more quickly and to a far larger audience.

A simple way to think about your idea is with Table 3.1. Ideas can be categorized into successful or unsuccessful and consensus or non-consensus. We naturally won't know whether an idea is successful or unsuccessful until after the fact, so the current focus is on distinguishing consensus from non-consensus ideas. Consensus ideas are those that the rest of the world shares, those that are obviously good and in

Table 3.1 How good is your idea?

	Consensus	Non-consensus
Successful	Some gains	Extraordinary gains
Unsuccessful	Lose everything	Lose everything

alignment with broadly held beliefs of how the world works. A non-consensus idea is one that most people likely think is ridiculous or impossible. Paul Graham,[10] co-founder of the renowned accelerator Y Combinator, has long held that the best ideas often sound like the stupidest ones when first presented – and that is a large part of why they end up being so successful (there are also many ideas that are simply bad, that's the hard part of investing).[11] This is part of why startups often receive scores of rejections for institutional fundraising before their first yes (sometimes even hundreds).[12]

Understanding why what you're proposing hasn't been done yet is a hugely important exercise for several reasons: first, it will help you understand what you have to prove in order to de-risk your venture (this is important both for you and for your potential investors); second, it will make rejection easier to accept and shake off – if everyone agrees and sees the value in what you're doing, then it will have already been done.

When it comes to your startup, identifying your non-consensus beliefs and then developing rapid and affordable ways to test them is crucial. Collecting indicators that those beliefs are accurate, and not merely misguided, is hugely important to the future success of your company, and one of the key differentiators between successful and unsuccessful founders. Unsuccessful founders often take their non-consensus belief for true and begin building their solution without collecting additional validation, instead collecting vanity metrics to convince themselves of their belief (humans are really good at doing this, it's called confirmation bias).

Not every brilliant idea has to be non-consensus. There could merely be an external factor in society that has changed, making your solution possible for the first time – whether it's the creation of a new platform or technology (think of the iPhone and the birth of the smartphone app), or perhaps legislative change. No matter what, there does have to be a strong '*why now*'. If there is no foundational non-consensus belief at the bedrock of your solution, it becomes a matter of speed and execution – and fortunately, one of the few major advantages startups have over giant competitors is that they're able to move much more quickly.

Notes

1 Desjardins, J (2019) How much data is generated each day? *World Economic Forum*, https://www.weforum.org/agenda/ 2019/04/how-much-data-is-generated-each-day-cf4bddf29f/ (archived at https://perma.cc/3REU-3QQ4)

2 There's an App for That, trademark details, https://trademarks. justia.com/779/80/there-s-an-app-for-77980556.html (archived at https://perma.cc/3K6S-SNU7)

3 Le Brouster, G (2018) TAM SAM SOM – what it means and why it matters, *The Business Plan Shop*, https://www. thebusinessplanshop.com/blog/en/entry/tam_sam_som (archived at https://perma.cc/F9ES-4MAA)

4 Fitzpatrick, R (2019) *The Mom Test: How to talk to customers and learn if your business is a good idea when everyone is lying to you*, CreateSpace

5 Economic Census Tables (2020) https://www.census.gov/ programs-surveys/economic-census/data/tables.html (archived at https://perma.cc/8NGF-HR34)

6 CBInsights (2021) Why Startups Fail: Top 20 Reasons, https:// www.cbinsights.com/research/startup-failure-reasons-top/ (archived at https://perma.cc/3C5N-QGYE)

7 Kahneman, D (2015) *Thinking, Fast and Slow*, Farrar, Straus and Giroux, New York

8 van Mulukom, V (2019) The secret to creativity – according to science, *The Conversation*, http://theconversation.com/the-secret-to-creativity-according-to-science-89592 (archived at https://perma.cc/ST4T-VAEK)

9 Boden, M (1995) Creativity and Unpredictability, *Stanford Humanities Review*, 4 (2), https://dl.acm.org/doi/abs/10.5555/212154.212171 (archived at https://perma.cc/R7PC-E745)

10 Graham, P (2013) Do things that don't scale, http://paulgraham.com/ds.html (archived at https://perma.cc/52T7-433S)

11 Lapowsky, I (2013) Paul Graham on building companies for fast growth, *Inc*, https://www.inc.com/magazine/201309/issie-lapowsky/how-paul-graham-became-successful.html (archived at https://perma.cc/K7C8-4L9K)

12 Allen, R (2017) 173 rejections while fundraising and we were considered successful, *Medium*, https://robbieallen.medium.com/175-rejections-while-fundraising-and-we-were-considered-successful-85eebe97fd65 (archived at https://perma.cc/952X-WATK)

04
Common causes of failure

There are many common mistakes when starting a business – those presented here are a fraction, which we've selected because we believe they pose the most risk to the viability of your venture. We'll discuss both practical and conceptual mistakes. The point is not to provide 'secret tips' or to convince you that by avoiding these errors you're guaranteeing yourself success. Avoiding these mistakes isn't necessarily difficult, but what's important is that you know where and why most mistakes are made so that you can critically evaluate your approach to avoid them. In addition, you have to be able to critically evaluate your actions *honestly* – most people are, unsurprisingly, really terrible at this. In order for anything in this chapter to be even remotely useful, you must be willing to recognize your flaws and actively remedy them as quickly as possible. Every human that has ever existed, especially those that like to call themselves entrepreneurs, are prone to self-deception, and it's particularly easy to do in the context of running a startup. When constantly on the verge of having their company fall apart, or constantly trying to find the motivation to keep going, entrepreneurs tend to resort to a bull-headed 'do it or die trying' mentality, or a 'the world doesn't understand, but they'll see, just wait' point of view. Ironically, this mentality is responsible for both some of the largest successes and the largest failures in the startup world. Self-awareness is critical. Now enough with the moralizing, let's get to it!

First mistake – rigidity

In Quinn's second year of university, he worked on a startup with a CEO who couldn't bear to give up on his vision of what the company's product should be, despite repeatedly receiving feedback from users that the product wasn't addressing their needs. He had an amazing team, significant funding, and he was generally an open-minded person, but he saw pivoting or adjusting the vision of the product as 'giving up'. The product in question was a mobile-first messaging application that aimed to provide drag-and-drop functionality with in-app communication and file management – think Slack and Google Drive combined, but for students as opposed to workplaces. While the tech was impressive, the CEO repeatedly pushed for the product not to be viewed as an app, but as an operating system. Despite repeated pushback on this, and recommendations to focus instead on building out a really effective user experience as a first and more manageable step, he continually invested in additional features in an effort to build more of an operating system-in-an-app. In the end, the company couldn't get students to use the app due to complaints of 'confusing user experience' and 'ugly user interface', which resulted in being unable to raise another round of funding, the company's funds drying up, and ultimately the startup shutting down.

On more than one occasion, the CEO claimed that the customers didn't know what they needed until they were shown – he was incorrect. Chapters 2 and 3 go into more depth about how to avoid this particular mistake.

To the credit of the CEO in question, this is perhaps one of the easiest mistakes to make and one of the most difficult to avoid. It is exceptionally hard to strike a balance between having sufficient belief in yourself and what you're building, and being receptive to criticism and feedback. The remedy is to ensure you're asking the right questions of your potential users. This takes a lot of practice and is something most of us are pretty bad at, particularly as founders – we're frequently too invested in the answer to ask an unbiased or non-leading question. Chapter 5 will cover this topic in much greater depth.

Second mistake – the passion myth

The second major mistake often occurs before people have even started down the path of creating a business. It's a mischaracterization responsible for a lot of people choosing and then later leaving entrepreneurship. We will call it the passion myth.

A routine search on Amazon will give you more than 1,300 business books on the topic of 'passion'. There surely isn't that much to say about it, and given this book's current trajectory, it is perhaps obvious at this point that we disagree with the generic recommendation of 'follow your passion and everything will work out'. In any job, there are aspects you will really enjoy as well as aspects you will detest. The point being, the notion that a job can or should invoke constant passion is a false one. Starting a business is no different. In what is a lovely irony, the word 'passion' derives its meaning from the root word 'pati-', Latin for 'suffer'. In its original usage, 'passion' was characterized as an external force that causes an individual to act in some way and suffer for it, often in a religious sense, for example the passion of Christ. Entrepreneurship is a lot more like the first translation of passion than the second.

Apart from the ironic interpretive shift from suffering to elation, we have two major complaints with the notion that 'passion' should define your career aspirations. First, the notion that a particular career is not worthy of pursuit if it does not instil individuals with a sense of euphoria is inherently problematic. The ability of a career to induce passion is often dependent on the narratives our society has woven around it. Professions like investment banking are illustrated in rose-tinted terminology with narratives of wealth, happiness and Wolf of Wall Street debauchery, while other careers like teaching are given little focus in the whirling stream of societal consciousness. The point is that the ability of a given role to induce passion often becomes an issue of culture rather than an issue of the merits of a particular profession in and of itself. Second, the satisfaction that comes with doing a job can often be found in its nuances, the small moments day to day that come together to make the job worth doing. In entrepreneurship, this idea is particularly important because it requires a lot of sacrifice and stress upfront in the *hope* (not guarantee) that there will be a payout down the road. Keep pushing long enough to find that success is often dependent on finding those moments day to day that make the job worth doing.

Third mistake – no market need

For the most part this has already been covered, but it bears repeating. *Build. For. Customers. You. Know. Exist.* In an analysis of more than 100 startup failures by the firm CB Insights, the number one reason for failure, accounting for 42 per cent of all failures, was having no market need.[1] 17 per cent of the startups failed because they built a user-unfriendly product. 14 per cent failed because they ignored customers. The previous chapter on getting started may make readers hesitate – it feels like a lot of work up front, before you've even nailed down a solution. That is on purpose. It takes time and effort to create a great idea and then validate its viability. The process isn't necessarily exciting or fun, but it does mean your company won't fail for the same reason more than half of the other startups do – and *that* is worth the trouble.

Fourth mistake – team composition

If the most common reason companies fail is because they don't build to address a market need, the second most common is having poor team composition. We'll go into this particular mistake in far more detail in Chapter 7, but it's worth mentioning briefly here. In the CB Insights report on startup failures, poor team composition was responsible for 23 per cent of all failures. In fact, team composition is so important that many venture capital firms and other investors can be quoted as saying that at the early stages of a company – in seed or pre-seed funding rounds (more on this in Chapter 11) – their investment decision is based more on the quality of the team than the idea itself. Seventy-three per cent of all startups will pivot their market focus, meaning that they've changed their target customer segment because their initial one didn't support their business as expected. With three-quarters of startups pivoting at some point, it would be foolish for seed-stage investors to focus too heavily on the business idea when it is likely that the idea will dramatically change in the near future. So instead, investors look for teams they think will be flexible and competent enough to handle a constantly changing startup, a team that has the skills to keep things running when everything is going unexpectedly.

So how should or shouldn't you build your team? First, you have to find a way to make the hard work fun or, at the very least, bearable. Because there's a lot of it. Consider implementing monthly team socials, where your team can interact with each other in a relaxed environment and get to know one another outside of work. Second, you need people to tell you when you're wrong and when you're right. Having people around you who will hold you accountable and will not simply agree with you by default is necessary in life, but especially in building a company. Encourage your team to point out any discernible flaws in your thinking on a consistent basis; when they genuinely have nothing to dispute, use this as a sense of confirmation that everyone is on board. Third, you can't do it all and you will need skills other than your own to be successful early on. Being in school is a perfect opportunity to meet others with different backgrounds and skill sets than your own. In fact, it's likely that you will never have such access to such a diverse talent pool ever again. Software and tech-focused startups have now cited software developers as more valuable than money, so having access to developers and technically competent team members through your university or school experiences can make or break your company.

Fifth mistake – losing focus

When people start a business, be it a B2B or B2C, or some combination of the two, there's a propensity to try to reach as many different customers as possible early on. It's intuitively appealing to do – the more customers your product aligns with or provides value for, the more potential buyers! Unfortunately, that is not how it usually (ever) plays out. Concentrating on a niche market segment early on allows you to focus your product or service to the needs of that customer group – doing so allows for a better product–market fit, and greatly increases your ability to gain traction early on. Understanding the market composition and the needs of a larger customer base is crucial for scaling later on, but when startups try to scale prematurely, they lose their ability to give customers a well-fit product and consequently limit their growth. So as long as you've selected a good problem to go about solving (see Chapter 2), there should be plenty of room for expansion after you've found initial success and gained stable traction. This is why choosing the right problem to focus on really matters. It's certainly more difficult than it sounds.

There's an important distinction between keeping focus and focusing too much. Often, crossing that line is motivated by efforts to avoid competitors. At the point at which there are no competitors, either you've focused on a marginal niche or you have a revolutionary solution; and it's usually pretty easy to tell the difference. The difference lies in asking how many people directly experience the problem you're looking to solve. A marginal niche would be you providing an app with one feature: for people to message each other 'Yo'. In that scenario, there are no competitors for a reason, as it doesn't actually solve a problem for people. On the other hand, truly revolutionary startups solve unsolved problems, and their competitors are usually indirect ones simply because their ideas aren't derivative, rather than because their market segment is too small to support competitors.

Sixth mistake – waiting too long

When you begin designing your solution, you'll quickly realize that it is endlessly improvable. There will never be a point at which your software is completely perfect, or your service or product exactly meets the needs of your customers. Similarly, you will never feel totally ready to go to market, given that there are always more features to add or improve upon. Waiting too long causes your motivation to wither away and gives your competitors an opportunity to gain the critical market share they need to put you out of business or keep you from ever really getting started on your idea in the first place.

There are several distinct problems that drive this hesitation, including working on too many different things, excessive perfectionism, not truly understanding the problem or your customers, and simply working too slowly. Michele Romanow (President of Clearco) says the success of a startup in its early years comes down to how fast its team executes and how quickly they iterate their product based on customer feedback. So how do you do this? There are a number of ways. For Swish, he uses calendar invites to set deadlines for himself and his team. He holds his team accountable for missing tasks and he expects his team to do the same for him. When Swish was building Surf, he started off building a non-functional prototype (also referred to as an MVP) so he could get user feedback immediately. The value of an MVP will be discussed in Chapter 5, but it's worth noting that doing this has helped Swish explain his ideas better to potential investors and advisors. For Quinn, he got started on Autumn by setting up meetings with his professors and friends. He told them about the problem, his proposed solution, and challenged whoever he met to question him. Any questions he could not answer gave him more areas to explore and do research on. No matter what you do, just know that taking small actions and holding yourself accountable to a timeline will always serve you better than waiting and thinking about all possible future roadblocks.

Student advantage

The odds are that you will not be dropping out like Swish to pursue your company, which means you likely have two to four years in an academic institution before you have the freedom to commit the majority of your efforts to your startup. This can be a really good thing – first, it forces you to take your time in setting the groundwork for your company so that you can launch once you have the flexibility to commit more fully. Second, while in school you are best positioned to iteratively improve your solution because you have access to a massive network of colleagues, academics and industry professionals. You can approach each of these individuals as a student looking to gain insight. Third, when you begin the process of customer acquisition, you have to be more selective – with the additional challenge of balancing school and your company, you are forced to evaluate your business model and customer segment to ensure you get it right the first time. This rigorous evaluation is nothing but a good thing for your company.

Note

1 CB Insights (2020) Why Startups Fail: Top 20 Reasons, https://www.cbinsights.com/research/startup-failure-reasons-top/ (archived at https://perma.cc/CY2J-7KGE)

05
Minimum viable product

Think about it. So many people have business ideas. If you went outside and you asked 10 people, 'What's the best business idea you have?' I can guarantee a majority of people would give you an answer. People have ideas but what separates them from entrepreneurs is *execution*. You need to take your idea and do something with it, and that's where having a minimum viable product comes into play.

What is an MVP?

A key element to entrepreneurial success is the ability to build your minimum viable product (MVP) incredibly fast. The MVP is a proof of the concept you're pitching to clients, investors, and partners. It's the most minimal version of your solution that demonstrates its core value. The faster you can deploy your MVP, the faster you can begin collecting information that tells you if you're on the right track. It's imperative that customers can engage with your idea in a tangible way. The single most significant piece of information you will collect is whether or not people actually use your MVP.

If people or businesses are actually willing to try your MVP it's a great early indicator that you're on the right track. It means you're solving a problem so crucial for your customers that they're willing to use an unfinished product. Giving early adopters the ability to play around with an initial iteration can possibly unearth some of the flaws in your product or service and this feedback will help mould the product into one that customers are comfortable using, helping your company gain early momentum and popularity among early adopters. Likewise, customers appreciate a company willing to integrate their preferences and suggestions, as they feel like they are a part of the development process and therefore attribute a sense of loyalty to your business.

Types of MVP

There are three main types of MVP you may want to consider: a landing page, an instructional MVP, or a Flintstone MVP.

Landing page MVP

Eventually, you will have one destination where you will drive people to in order to sell them your finished product. For most types of business, this is likely to be a very simple website – a landing page. So, why not create it *before* you have a finished product? Having a live landing page, even if only for your testers, can capture extremely valuable information. For example:

- conversion rates (if your potential customers aren't in the same country as you);

- pricing feedback (is your product too expensive – are people dropping off before they commit to buy? Or is it too inexpensive – maybe they're jumping on the idea and making multiple orders, or maybe they're *not* buying because they don't trust the quality of your product?);

- email addresses (for future mailing lists).

A functional landing page might even allow you to build up pre-orders as well as increase and demonstrate demand... all without investing any money into making the product!

Landing page MVPs can enhance customers' perception of the brand as it's often the first means of contact between the brand and its audience. These MVPs legitimize the business because all it takes is a simple online search to discover the company's MVP and unique value proposition. Information is at the hands of the customer who wants to access it, and so this MVP is best used when customers are driven to the landing page, rather than using it solely as an idle vehicle to attract customers. One disadvantage to note is that there will be people who access the page without clicking on the button to purchase or input their information for further communication, leaving you with no definitive reason why they chose not to do so.

Instructional MVP

An instructional MVP allows you to show off the basic features and principles of the idea, as well as what it intends to do, by asking customers to sign up to try it for themselves. By doing this, you can learn a lot about the perceived value of the idea from customer interest. Numbers don't lie, and if zero customers sign up you can iterate to a new idea without wasting time or money on an unwanted product. When considering this type of MVP, it's important to understand that your sign-ups are not directly correlated to your sales, that each new registrant is merely a demonstration of interest in the product, and not yet a guaranteed paying customer for your business.

Flintstone MVP

This aims to create an MVP that gives the *illusion* of a fully functional product, but relies on manpower to deliver the finished solution (like the foot-powered car from *The Flintstones* cartoon). It's a model that works well for services: to customers, your product seems fully developed but on the back end *you're* pulling all the strings to make it happen. One big advantage of this MVP type is how closely you can interact with customers, moving forward with the idea once you have garnered a positive response. This close interaction with a customer is far less susceptible to social biases that may occur when a customer is knowingly interacting with the founder face to face. This objective data is vital in understanding how a customer genuinely receives your product or service. The Flintstone MVP can typically save you money in the short term as it pays a human to perform tasks behind the scenes. This process mimicry can even allow you to gauge how a fully fledged system would work prior to investing an extensive amount of resources while waiting for the automated process to function. One potentially derailing requirement of this MVP is that it obligates the human behind the scenes to do near-flawless work, which can pose a challenge for the founder to find others with the same knowledge and skillset (or otherwise bear the entire burden on their own).

CASE STUDY   DoorDash

A Flintstone MVP is how US-based food delivery app DoorDash
started: co-founders Tony and Stanley would take food orders
through their website for customers' favourite restaurants…
then they would literally order the food from the restaurants
themselves, and deliver it to their customers' doors. DoorDash is
now a fully functioning, multi-state operation, providing gig-
economy employment and partnering with a range of businesses
across the United States.

Examples of MVPs

Amazon – a simple, yet well-thought-out MVP

Amazon wasn't always the e-commerce behemoth that is
currently the largest retailer in the world, 25 years after its
origination. The company did not enter the market with
Amazon Web Services and Amazon Prime, the services that
are its most profitable today. Instead, founder Jeff Bezos
started the company with a service that may come as a sur-
prise to most: shipping books to customers. If you wanted to
purchase a book, you could do so by searching for a title on
amazon.com, 'Earth's biggest bookstore', which would then
ship you your book at a competitively low cost.[1] This product category was clever in retrospect: simple to buy, to ship,
and was fairly inexpensive to the end customer.[2] An online

intermediary (a party that transacts between customer and distributor) for books is how Amazon began, and it was this MVP that contributed to its monstrous success in selling other product categories (which is now just about everything) later on. This is because, as any good MVP does, they were able to harness a great deal of feedback while buying books from distributors and shipping them to customers. This constant feedback loop gave Amazon the knowledge and confidence to repeatedly iterate, each time with a new product offering of some sort, or a more streamlined process of operation. The lesson for entrepreneurs: have a well-thought-out strategy for your MVP, which involves keeping it simple. Remember, your MVP is not your final product. Your final product is the result of continuous iteration through harvesting loads of customer feedback.

Netflix – the metamorphosis of an imperfect MVP

Still worried about an imperfect MVP being fatal to the success of your business? To disprove this misconception, we take a look at a company that has experienced undeniable success: Netflix. Before it achieved about 158 million paid memberships globally,[3] the online entertainment streaming service, which originated all the way back in 1997, underwent several iterations both on a product development basis and from a brand image standpoint. Just take a look at its landing page from 2002 to see what we mean.[4]

What you will find is a single webpage outlining the benefits of renting DVD movies with Netflix: 'Super selection, free and fast home delivery, no due dates or late fees, and free shipping' are emblazoned within the first few lines of the page. Along with the fee per month, and a contact number listed for potential customer enquiries, the rest of the page features an in-depth explanation of what 'cookies' are on your computer, and how you can activate them in order to access Netflix's catalogue of DVDs. That's it!

An MVP is intended to simply showcase your idea in a way that can demonstrate its potential for customers, intriguing them to the point that they want to give it a try. It's vital to understand that an MVP is not the permanent state of your product, but rather a launchpad designed to propel you forward in terms of customer awareness and growth.

Airbnb – don't overthink it

Still not convinced you need to create an MVP? We're sure you've heard of Airbnb, or maybe even used the service yourself. Before it became the premier online marketplace for facilitating temporary accommodation across 100,000 cities worldwide, Airbnb was built on the premise of one particular need: a place to stay. Founders Joe Gebbia and Brian Chesky wanted to launch their business but were low on funds, so low they were struggling to pay rent! To mend this situation, they sought a way to make use of the idle space within their apartment. The pair noticed a frequent problem within the accommodation market, which was the high cost and degree of difficulty in finding hotel rooms, especially around the time of a large event in an area. A pressing question still remained in their minds: would complete strangers be willing to pay them to stay at their residence? When a design conference was taking place near their apartment in San Francisco, they wasted no time in trying to test this question. They didn't have millions of dollars in the bank to promote Airbnb and show the world how great their idea was. Instead, they had an empty room, some air mattresses and the camera on their iPhone.[5] They launched their MVP with the resources they had, and the result was a basic website with photos of their unoccupied bedroom. This basic and direct approach enabled them to create a testable offering in the shortest amount of time. They went directly to market and proved the concept, signing up three paying guests.[6] These guests were able to get an early experience of what the founders (who acted as the sellers) had to offer at the time: an air mattress, free Wi-Fi, and breakfast. In doing so, Gebbia and Chesky were able to spend lots of time with their customers, getting plenty of feedback and a better idea of what guests were looking for in their service. These initial insights and customer interactions were instrumental in the creation of Airbnb, as the founders were able to garner quality customer feedback and build customer loyalty in the meanwhile. Today the company is valued at $38 billion,[7] and it all started with a basic MVP, a website with a few photos. *Stop overthinking it and get moving!*

The value of an MVP

An MVP is not an end goal. It's also not a method to maximize revenues. An MVP is a *stepping stone* that allows you to build, measure and learn. When creating and developing your MVP, there are four main objectives you should focus on:

- developing a user base or clientele;
- collecting user data;

- generating user feedback;
- improving your product or service.

When developing an MVP, you have the opportunity to connect deeply with your potential users. As Brian Chesky said, 'Build something 100 people love, not 1 million people kind of like'.[8] Your 100 early adopters and true fans will vouch for you and amplify your business through word of mouth and direct referrals, the *best* kind of marketing.

CASE STUDY   Slack

Slack, the SaaS company that unifies your entire company's communications to improve workflow, places a heavy importance on listening to customer feedback; CEO Stewart Butterfield credits much of their success to this. Slack takes user feedback any way they can get it, from support buttons embedded in the application to scrolling through Twitter comments for good and bad feedback.[9] Listening to customer feedback, especially from early users, allowed them to implement small changes that had big impacts, and Butterfield believes 'Beta-tester feedback is crucial to finding those little oversights in a product design'.[10] Customer feedback is your golden ticket to building your MVP into a successful product: implement it and you will create happy users who willingly recommend you to others.

Customer feedback is king

The benefits of customer feedback and loyalty are solidified by most successful companies that use a minimum viable product to test their offering with a few willing customers, before showing their final iteration to the public. This is a commonly understood way of thinking that is not often executed well in the real product landscape. Even companies that have enjoyed a great deal of success are prone to making fundamental hiccups. To illustrate this, we look at the peculiar case of the Google Glass. The product was equipped with augmented reality capabilities that allowed users to send and receive messages, take pictures, and record videos in an urban setting, all through eyeglasses on their face.[11] Google applications like Gmail, Google Maps and Translate were all built in, with news and social media network sharing also being marketed features. Being a Google product, it attracted all sorts of hype, with the company launching various dazzling videos to introduce the interactive and wearable technology to the public. The initial version of the Google Glass made its debut in 2013, complete with its full array of features. Criticism quickly erupted when users of the product posed many concerns for other citizens within the area. Several complaints highlighting that users could be recording unknowing passersby drew issues of privacy.[12] Concerns regarding safety were also raised as users were wearing the device while driving, an evident distraction. The device was even a popular target among hackers, a serious threat given the access to personal data and facial recognition.

Today, after a failed attempt with 8,000 users in which estimates suggest the device cost Google hundreds of millions of dollars,[13] the company has iterated the product away from the consumer market and towards industrial use. The Google Glass example demonstrates that you have no true way of knowing whether or not your product will work for users until they have the opportunity to interact with it. Rather than assume that the product is viable, a simple MVP is used to test and validate the viability of the product. Do not build for the largest relevant market but instead, start by building and testing for a select few users. It will not be as easy for you to bounce back as it was for Google!

How do you design an MVP?

Now that we have established the benefits of creating an MVP, what are some best practices to go about designing your initial prototype? It could be as straightforward as putting pencil to paper and creating a visual mind map of what you want the first version of your product to look like and how it will be built, just like Swish did when he began creating Surf. If you're creating a physical product, it helps to go out and gather as much information as possible that will be relevant to the production of the initial version of your product.

Imagine that you want to start a business around selling t-shirts. How do you design your MVP? The process begins by thinking about who you want to sell your t-shirts to. What is your niche or target customer profile? Keep your target customer in mind throughout the design process, and put yourself in their shoes. Then, you would start sketching out what you want your t-shirt to look like. How do you want it to feel? What do you want the consumer to think when they see your t-shirt for the first time? How the t-shirt looks is ultimately the foundation of the business, so its design will determine whether or not someone will buy it. Next, you want to think about where you will source your t-shirts, since a tangible version of your t-shirt will be used to show potential customers. This involves conducting research, getting on the phone with various shirt distributors to obtain quotes for a batch. How many t-shirts do you want to produce for the first test with customers? It's important to consider the degree to which you believe the quality of the shirt will matter to your customer when choosing a supplier. Selling a t-shirt that shrinks or rips after only a few wears may permanently ruin your reputation. Once you have your t-shirts, the last step would be to print your design. Contact local printing companies to assess how expensive a process this would be. Are there companies that offer to source and print t-shirts? Investigating all possible routes will inevitably save you money. After completing all of these steps, you have designed your MVP. Now what? Go out and validate it! Remember that starting with a few people in your audience is necessary before branching out to the larger acceptable market.

Designing your MVP is different when creating an application, and there are multiple platforms that will help you create a visualization for your MVP in this form. Invision, Balsamiq, Mockingbird and Unbounce are particularly useful as platforms that enable you to design and build out a wireframe or prototype.

Your goal in building a wireframe is to provide a walkthrough to any potential client or investor. They should be able to click through the product and see all the various pages you want included.

If you're building a physical product, take as little of your budget as possible to develop the first iteration of that product. It doesn't have to be functional; it just has to be something that provides a clear picture to people of how the product would be used. For example, if you were developing an armband that could track the physical analytics of your arm during stress, for an MVP you could build the armband and show where it would go, how light it would be and what it would look like. That picture is a lot clearer than just including words in a pitch and hoping people can see exactly what you have in mind.

If you're building a service-based company, you're golden! If you're offering a service, you can literally go outside, knock on a few doors, and get instant feedback from random people on whether they would purchase your service. For example, if you want to start a local lawn mowing service, go out door-knocking and see if people are interested in paying for your services. If they are – voila! You have created demand for your service and brought in your first customers.

Don't spend too much time developing your MVP though: we would suggest spending no more than three weeks to construct it before showing the world. Eric Ries, author of *The Lean Startup*, put it best when he said, 'A minimum viable product is a version of a new product which allows a team to collect the maximum amount of validated learning about customers with the least effort'.[14] You don't want to waste loads of time and resources on this – the key is to get feedback, sooner rather than later.

Striking the balance

There are a few things to keep in mind when building your MVP. You're building your idea into a *minimum* viable product: a product with just the *core features*. A common pitfall we've seen among entrepreneurs developing their MVPs is to chase after the 'perfect product'. They try to offer every feature, leading to excess spending and a complicated MVP that overwhelms their potential customers. On the other extreme, don't mistake the goal of creating a minimum *viable* product with aiming to create the most bare-bones, crude version of the product. You should aim to create a product with enough features to carry users through the journey and goals they anticipate achieving – it may be minimum, but it's still got to be viable!

To understand what it takes to design your MVP, look into the brilliant minds of some of the best product designers in the world today. James Dyson is a British inventor and industrial designer. He has become a household name for being the founder of Dyson, the company that makes the bagless vacuum cleaner and bladeless fan, among other products. In an interview with *Inc*, he shares that product design is not about striking a creative idea, but rather an unwavering persistence that involves moving past the failures you encounter. 'I made 5,127 prototypes of my vacuum before I got it right. There were 5,126 failures. But I learned from each one. That's how I came up with a solution. So I don't mind failure'.[15] Upon entering product design for your MVP, you need to understand that you will not hit the nail on the head within the first, second or third attempts. Going further, it's accepting this failure as a reality, and being comfortable with it, that will inevitably keep you mentally focused on the process. Dyson also highlights the importance of product iteration here, by obtaining feedback from each previous version.

Another figure in the product design Hall of Fame is longtime Nike designer Tinker Hatfield, creator of the infamous Michael Jordan signature models. In an interview with *GQ*, he says how he created the classic Air Max 1: 'Good design is appropriate for its time and place. An important aspect of design that we look at on a regular basis (is) how far do you take anything before people no longer understand it? And if they don't understand it, they might not like it.'[16] Hatfield uncovers the universal truth of product design here, that ultimately the customer gives the final verdict. You cannot be stubborn about the design of your product. Instead, you must be willing to sacrifice your personal vision if you're stepping too far outside what your customer is willing to accept. How do you know whether or not your target customer will accept your design? Share your MVP with them! Taking customer feedback into consideration, including what your customers' preferences are, is how your product moves past an MVP and becomes something that customers will spend money on (more on this in Chapter 6). Hatfield considered this when he decided to release the Air Max 1 instead of the Air Max Zero, a model that he claims was 'literally too ahead of its time for us to produce'.[17]

Perhaps Amanda Linden, Director of Product Design at Facebook, describes the design process of an early-stage product best, stating, '... great products come from a continuous process of building and refining, not just building and building more.'[18] The key to product design is in ensuring that current aspects of the product operate perfectly, rather than desperately attempting to add more unnecessary aspects to the existing product. In the case of early product design, less is more and a keen focus on the fundamental aspects of the product will save you a lot of time and energy.

What is the cost of an MVP?

To build out your MVP and test it with customers, you will need to find a way to finance the production of your product. You can pay for the MVP upfront, like our t-shirt example in which you could choose to pay the t-shirt distributor out of pocket. Another way to cover the cost of your MVP is to raise a sum of money from early investors to get off the ground. Platforms such as Kickstarter are known for crowd-funding, where the public pitches in money to projects and product ideas that they would like to see come to fruition. Oculus, the company behind the famous Oculus Rift virtual reality headset (which was later bought by Facebook), is an example of a success story that was initially funded by Kickstarter.[19] Raising money can even be as straightforward as asking your friends and family to help you turn your MVP into a reality, although we realize how uncomfortable this can be. A third option to consider, especially when your MVP is an application, is opting to relinquish a portion of 'sweat equity' to developers in exchange for building your MVP for no upfront payment. This form of equity relates to contribution in terms of labour, rather than financial capital, allowing developers to hold a stake in the business as a result of their time and effort. You must seek developers who have an interest and belief in your business long-term.

Table 5.1 shows a concise comparison of each of the three financing options.

Table 5.1 MVP financing options

Financing Your MVP	PROS	CONS
Paying developers upfront	• Don't need to give up any equity • Receive a functional prototype that will entice early customers or allow for fundraising on better terms	• Can be expensive and you cannot recoup the costs if things do not work out later (ie if people do not like your end product)
Fundraising	• You have money to play around with • Not only can you cover your development costs but you can also hire one or two salespeople or invest some money into advertising	• Sacrificing equity before you have established product/market fit (ie you do not yet know whether or not your concept will satisfy your end consumer)
Sweat equity (bringing developers onboard team)	• Helps in the future because if you need to make iterations, you can go to the same developer and make changes quickly • Having a technical lead is something investors look for	• Giving up equity • Uncertain whether or not the developer will remain in your team for the long run

Notes

1 Cakebread, C (2017) Amazon launched 22 years ago this week – here's what shopping on Amazon was like back in 1995, *Business Insider*, https://www.businessinsider.com/amazon-opened-22-years-ago-see-the-business-evolve-2017-7 (archived at https://perma.cc/CR2M-BV97)

2 Eakin, S (2018) Amazon is huge because it started with a great MVP, *Entrepreneur*, https://www.entrepreneur.com/article/308707 (archived at https://perma.cc/XS3X-9NW3)

3 Hayes, D (2019) New Netflix subscriber and revenue figures underscore boom outside U.S, *Deadline*, https://deadline.com/2019/12/new-netflix-subscriber-and-revenue-figures-underscore-boom-outside-u-s-1202810784/ (archived at https://perma.cc/HH7R-JAAY)

4 Wayback Machine, Netflix Landing Page 2002, https://web.archive.org/web/20021202120616/http://www.netflix.com/entryTrap.html#nc4 (archived at https://perma.cc/87EL-D8K3)

5 Mendoza, J (2019) Airbnb's app success story: A solid MVP, *Fueled*, https://fueled.com/blog/airbnb-mvp/ (archived at https://perma.cc/GR44-7WNB)

6 Ibid

7 Schleifer, T (2019) Airbnb sold some common stock at a $35 billion valuation, but what is the company really worth? *Vox*, https://www.vox.com/2019/3/19/18272274/airbnb-valuation-common-stock-hoteltonight (archived at https://perma.cc/LG3G-H949)

8 Shontell, A (2013) The best advice Airbnb CEO Brian Chesky ever received, *Business Insider*, https://www.businessinsider.com/the-best-advice-airbnb-ceo-brian-chesky-ever-received-2013-1 (archived at https://perma.cc/8ZKY-7W67)

9   Clifford, C (2019) Slack CEO Stewart Butterfield's tweet reveals a critical component to the company's success, *CNBC*, https://www.cnbc.com/2019/06/20/slack-ceo-butterfields-tweet-shows-key-component-to-companys-success.html (archived at https://perma.cc/9BZD-FQ8K)

10   Fast Company (2015) Slack's founder on how they became a $1 billion company in two years, https://www.fastcompany.com/3041905/slacks-founder-on-how-they-became-a-1-billion-company-in-two-years?utm_source=join1440&utm_medium=email&utm_placement=etcetera (archived at https://perma.cc/7LR6-ZBLK)

11   Satell, G (2019) Here's what most people get wrong about minimum viable products, *Digital Tonto*, https://www.digitaltonto.com/2019/heres-what-most-people-get-wrong-about-minimum-viable-products/ (archived at https://perma.cc/9PX4-XJZV)

12   Ibid

13   Bajarin, T (2015) The debacle of Google Glass, *Vox*, https://www.vox.com/2015/5/12/11562546/the-debacle-of-google-glass (archived at https://perma.cc/P5EV-ZPVX)

14   Ries, E (2009) Minimum Viable Product: a guide, *Startup Lessons Learned*, http://www.startuplessonslearned.com/2009/08/minimum-viable-product-guide.html (archived at https://perma.cc/23P9-TY9V)

15   Brandon, J (2016) James Dyson on how to invent insanely popular products, *Inc.com*, https://www.inc.com/john-brandon/james-dyson-on-how-entrepreneurs-need-to-innovate-not-just-invent.html?cid=search (archived at https://perma.cc/4UP5-PT46)

16   Woolf, J (2017) Meet the mastermind who designed your favorite Nikes, *GQ*, https://www.gq.com/story/tinker-hatfield-interview-steph-curry-nike?mbid=social_twitter (archived at https://perma.cc/P34J-3N43)

17   Ibid

18 Linden, A (2016) What does it take to enable great product design? *Medium*, https://medium.com/bridge-collection/what-does-it-take-to-enable-great-product-design-7a5c1abccfc8 (archived at https://perma.cc/S58D-7AZ2)

19 Chafkin, M (2017) Why Facebook's $2 billion bet on Oculus Rift might one day connect everyone on Earth, *Vanity Fair*, https://www.vanityfair.com/news/2015/09/oculus-rift-mark-zuckerberg-cover-story-palmer-luckey (archived at https://perma.cc/Q8XJ-V67B)

06
Testing and marketing your MVP

Product testing

Once you've built an MVP, you'll be ready for a test.

How do you do that? Sign up people for free, put flyers out, buy Facebook advertisements, hire your younger sibling to go door-knocking, do whatever it takes to get people to see the MVP. While you're showing your MVP, it's crucial to note down the feedback you're getting, especially if you're showing it to people you anticipate will invest later on. Investors want to feel like they were a part of the process. It makes them feel more connected to your company and will make you appear coachable and as someone they can work with. That is why we suggest not just doing one round of feedback but several. The more data you can give yourself (customer interest, customer pain points, etc), the better off you will be.

Go out to people and get their feedback, then go back to that same group a few weeks later. When you go back to them, ask them to provide you with more concrete and specific commentary on whether they think your idea and business model is viable. Would they put money into it? Would they purchase your product or service over others?

Responding to feedback

Building an MVP is all about finding the right balance between your offer to the customer and what the customer really needs. You're testing to see whether your belief that there is a demand for your product is validated by consumers. Pay attention to every side: the creation of your MVP will increase your understanding in the business and marketing side as well as the technical product side. You should keep an open mind to all kinds of feedback, but here are some points to get you started.

Marketing-type ideas:

- Can you conduct and analyse customer surveys?
- Can you gather and analyse data through various social media platforms?
- What are your marketing best practices?
- What is producing the best results?

Technical/product ideas:

- Can you test and execute key design and functionality features?
- What do customers react well to?
- What could they live without?
- What are your idea's unique attributes?

Don't be afraid to change direction

You're investing both your time and money into creating this business, so if there are any red flags, address them before going any further. This is the real point of the testing – helping investors feel involved will be worthless if your final product has problems that you ignored.

What are your testers telling you? Could your product be tweaked, developed, or improved? Is the product even viable? Perhaps once you start testing, this idea doesn't actually have legs. No matter how tempting, don't fool yourself and romanticize a particular business idea as 'the one'. As an entrepreneur, this won't be your only idea. You will always have business ideas, because the way you see the world is by the problems in it rather than the solutions – so don't get stuck on one idea at the expense of ignoring feedback. Executing a failing business plan is always a losing strategy that will leave you feeling heartbroken and frustrated.

Marketing your MVP

Choosing the correct channels to promote your MVP depends on the type of business you're building. Your marketing efforts vary depending on whether you're providing a product, a service, or a software application.

Marketing for a product can be done using a two-fold strategy:

- Give samples to key influencers or local leaders. See if any of these people are willing to provide a testimonial or do a video review.

- Attend local events and bring samples of your products with you! This is not a scalable strategy but it can be very effective early on – many entrepreneurs find showcasing their product and getting feedback from users in person is one of the best ways to truly understand what is missing in their product.

Marketing for a service business can be done using a three-fold strategy:

- Firstly and most effectively is word of mouth among your friends and family. The data information firm Nielsen reports that an astounding 92 per cent of consumers believe the recommendations of their family and friends more than they do regular advertising.[1] This is because you're constantly influenced by the suggestions of those around you when making decisions. Clearly, a carpool service company, for example, can greatly benefit from implementing this form of promotion, but how can word of mouth be executed so that both parties can benefit? Consider giving your friends and family (your first clients) a referral code, which will provide them with 50 per cent off their next ride if they get a friend to try out your service. A referral programme like this can create a domino effect of new clients, with each new rider obtaining the incentive to spread the message about your business.

- Secondly, move promotions online through the use of advertisements on social media platforms. This may seem like simple advice, but the key to successful implementation of this technique is to keep your ads hyper-focused within your city and local area. If you're providing your carpooling service in Toronto, you would not find it necessary to have your ads pop up online in Winnipeg. You want to narrow your online advertisements so that the customer segment within your local region, those who will access your services, are able to see them.

- Thirdly, similar to promoting a product, take your promotional efforts offline. This means attending events (eg trade shows, expos etc) related to your industry happening in your area. Setting up booths at these events to provide live demonstrations, information, and to simply meet your potential clients can go a long way in gaining exposure for your company. Consider your hypothetical carpooling service. An intriguing example of offline marketing is getting involved in the music scene. Music festivals are typically held in outer cities and desolate areas. Consequently, music fanatics travel in groups to get to these sites, contributing to their overall experience when attending festivals. By attending these festivals yourself, you can find these music enthusiasts and tell them about your carpooling service, promoting your business to potential clients who might have never heard of your business otherwise.

Promoting an application

Maybe you're instead considering building an application, and are looking for the appropriate marketing channels to spark interest from consumers. Since your software application is based online (be it web or mobile), creating social media advertisements would be an adequate way to get people to take notice of your app. It's not enough that people see your ad while scrolling through Instagram; you should be more interested in whether or not people opt to click in or transfer over to the next phase of information (your website or the app store to download the application). These conversions are how you can gauge how effective your ads are on social media, based on whether people want to learn more about your app. If you're not seeing any real conversion from your social media ads, you may want to consider how engaging your ads are or how well you're presenting the value of your app to the average person. Going further, app-based businesses can experience a lot of growth when providing value upfront by establishing partnerships. An example of this is how food delivery apps like Foodora are able to convince restaurants to offer certain discounts to customers. The restaurant benefits because they gain exposure to customers through this new vehicle, while the influx of customers get to enjoy the discount on their orders. Meanwhile, your food delivery app generates the nearly unquantifiable benefit of obtaining early users that will test out your app. Another example of providing value upfront as a channel of promotion is what Surf demonstrated with its early users. In its beta stage, the company would provide initial users with a best practices guide when they would come on board and try, download, and test out the app. This presentation of value upfront enabled Surf to build more meaningful relationships with their early beta users, who in turn provided the company with pertinent feedback about their app.

Measuring success

We've discussed the importance of utilizing several rounds of customer feedback to iterate and reiterate your product to the point that it will best satisfy the needs of the market. The next stage is to confidently measure how well we are doing in the process. It's vital for every business to establish specific key performance indicators (KPIs) that you believe will be of significance.[2] One good place to start is analysing the engagement of customers. This will certainly vary based on the platform you choose, but it's necessary in order to realize the current value of your MVP and to forecast what it will be worth to customers. Look at the feature flow of the user, which is the features of your product that are most frequently used and most valuable to your customers. Studying this will shed light on other features that are less important to users, helping you to narrow down the aspects of your product that truly resonate with customers, and concentrate on these core functions. Another KPI for measuring MVP success is how much time a user spends with your MVP. Is the time spent enjoyable for the user, or is it taking them too long to navigate through the MVP? You may also consider another KPI as whether or not the user is getting to the main benefit of your product quickly enough. Ideally, you want your customer to get to this core function or benefit within the first minute of interaction with the product. You will likely not be satisfied if your product is used once and never again, so understanding how many times a customer checks back on your MVP is also imperative in measuring its success. These KPIs rely on your ability to extract insights from your customer while they interact with your product. Companies including Surf allow you to understand the people who interact and engage with your products most, giving you the ability to focus your attention on specific customers for product insights. Once we can identify who our early adopters are, it's common practice to interview them and use our KPIs as a basis for how our MVP is performing.

Get started now

Maybe you're reading this chapter and still feel like you have no idea where to start in creating your MVP. But here's the thing: it's not about being *fancy*, it's about *execution*. As an entrepreneur, what separates you isn't your ability to create the 'perfect product'. Instead, it's getting to market first and making improvements! Don't worry about creating the most beloved product on the market, or getting it exactly right the first time... just *do it*. For some more inspiration, here are examples of successful companies that did just that.

Dropbox – get creative

Let's take a look at Dropbox, the cloud-based solution for sharing and storing files. Although it's now valued at over US $12bn,[3] when they were just getting going, that was far from the case. They needed a way to see if customers would pay for their service in order to validate the viability of their idea to investors and gain traction. However, development of the actual product would take a lot of time and money, two things they did not have. So, they created an MVP. Their MVP was a three-minute video that explained the concept of Dropbox. This simple video increased customer sign-ups by 1,400 per cent,[4] proving the market demand before they even launched, and giving investors the assurance they needed. The buzz they created with their MVP helped them capture the attention of Steve Jobs, and raise $250 million in investment![5]

The lesson here is to act quickly and be resourceful. When the founders realized it would not be possible to create a prototype of the product, they used this roadblock as an opportunity to get creative and appeal to consumers through a video.

Customer feedback

Geoff Ralston and Michael Seibel from Y Combinator suggest that you should be doing two things as a founder: building your product and talking to users.[6] Particularly for those of you at the point of deploying your MVP and looking for users, it's important to be talking directly with as many users as you possibly can. It's uncomfortable, it's awkward, it's frustrating, and it can be slow. But talking directly to users is the single most valuable thing you can do in the early stages of your company. It would be far easier to run $15 in Facebook ads and get 1,000 page views and perhaps a couple of new users, but you will have lost the opportunity to really understand those users and why they're interested in what you're making. It is often the case that solutions are adopted for reasons entirely different than those assumed by the founders. When you get sign-ups through social media ads, it is far more difficult to confirm whether the specific value you're looking to provide users is necessarily the value they are yielding from your product or service.

While building Autumn, we found that the appeal to individuals was less related to the value of being able to track their psychological well-being as we had first assumed, and more as a tool for performance improvement in the workplace. This difference in perceived value meant that we prioritized features that focused on helping users monitor how psychological well-being affects performance rather than on building tools to measure other psychological states. It meant weeks spent building something users actually wanted instead of something we thought they wanted.

Particularly early on, the key is not to get as many users as possible, but to get users that truly love your product, and to understand why they love your product and how you can continue to build on those strengths. So, hold off on ads and instead go out and speak with your users. At Autumn, we went to a WeWork nearby and went up to people in the kitchen and asked if we could chat briefly. The only metric we measured for ourselves early on was how many users we'd talked to, not how much revenue we had (at that point it was none), nor how many users we actually had, nor how many features we pushed.

Albert Einstein is sometimes credited with saying, 'Insanity is doing the same thing over and over again and expecting different results.' MVPs are immensely helpful in garnering this feedback and attracting the different perspectives that will ultimately yield additional feedback and identify new ways to improve your solution (whether the results are good or bad, this is a sign of progression). When gathering customers, it is important that you're asking them the right questions so that you're learning about your MVP as much as humanly possible. Tristan Kromer, author of *Grasshopper Herder*, a lean startup blog, once tweeted, 'Customers without feedback is like drinking salt water. Satisfying when dying of thirst but still deadly.'[7] Customers and feedback must go hand in hand; it is simply not enough for your family and friends to be wearing your t-shirt because they support you. Ask anyone who has spent time with your product open-ended but relevant questions so that you can reap useful insights about your initial prototype.

Here is a list of potential questions to ask:

- What is the first thing you would do with this product?
- What features stand out to you?
- Which features would you not use?
- Do you find navigating this product intuitive?
- What do you think is the product's intended purpose?
- Are you willing to buy this product right now?

If the answer is no to the last question, proceed by allowing them to imagine that they had the power to make any changes to the product. What addition to the product would make you want to buy it? The key here is to unlock sincere and objective thoughts that the customer has about your MVP.[8] Remove yourself from the equation to realize the relationship between the product and the user.

Often, our hesitation in sharing our MVP with the market is due to a general insecurity that stems from possible poor reception. What if the market does not see the value in my product? There are two ways to think about and move forward with this situation: (1) this is precisely what an MVP is for! If my MVP is not well received, what are the misconceptions that people have about my product? How can I convey my idea more accurately through my various channels of communication? Consider another iteration of your product to fix these concerns, or perhaps a pivot to another use case. Another thing to realize in order to overcome this hesitation is that (2) if I continue to wait to release my MVP, there is a possibility that another company can introduce a similar idea or concept to the market instead. Your competition will not wait for you to act!

Notes

1 Anon (2015) Recommendations from friends remain most credible form of advertising among consumers; branded websites are the second-highest-rated form, *Nielsen*, https://www.nielsen.com/eu/en/press-releases/2015/recommendations-from-friends-remain-most-credible-form-of-advertising/ (archived at https://perma.cc/AB5L-TF6X)

2 Robles, P (2012) The what and how of minimum viable products, *Econsultancy*, https://econsultancy.com/the-what-and-how-of-minimum-viable-products/ (archived at https://perma.cc/3T93-R43S)

3 Anon (2021) Dropbox Net Worth 2016-2021 I DBX, *Macrotrends*, https://www.macrotrends.net/stocks/charts/DBX/dropbox/net-worth (archived at https://perma.cc/92WM-J4F5)

4 Chang, L-X (2019) The Dropbox Story, Retold, *Issuu*, https://issuu.com/jumpstartmagazine/docs/april-issuu-final/s/94479 (archived at https://perma.cc/LGF3-RQ64)

5 Yakowicz, W (2013) Why Dropbox's founders said no to Steve Jobs, *Inc.com*, https://www.inc.com/will-yakowicz/why-dropbox-founders-said-no-steve-jobs.html (archived at https://perma.cc/3M5H-F9W6)

6 Ralston, G and Seibel, M (2018) YC's essential startup advice: becoming a founder, early stage, talking to users, *Y Combinator*, https://www.ycombinator.com/library/4D-yc-s-essential-startup-advice (archived at https://perma.cc/B2L9-A9CR)

7 Kromer, T (2014) How to build a minimum viable product? *Kromatic*, https://kromatic.com/blog/the-four-parts-of-a-minimum-viable-product/ (archived at https://perma.cc/MN5U-46BE)

8 Lanoue, S (2015) 4 reasons why you should user test your product early and often, *UserTesting*, https://www.usertesting.com/blog/4-reasons-why-you-should-user-test-your-product (archived at https://perma.cc/L9FX-2H5Y)

07
Development

The development of your company comes in two forms: developing your product and developing your vision.

Developing your product

It's time to take your MVP to the next stage of development and create the final iteration. Throughout the process, you have created your MVP, validated it, and gathered feedback and data from users. At this point, you have broken the MVP down into the simplest version by asking yourself three fundamental questions:

- Does this problem exist?
- Is the problem important enough?
- Can we solve the problem?

To create the simplest version of your MVP, it is extremely important that you focus on the core features; the features that you cannot do without. What is the 20 per cent of the work that will generate 80 per cent of the outcome? By figuring this out, it will become extremely clear to you which features of your MVP are vital and which ones are 'nice-to-haves' that can be implemented after you're established. You must now prioritize features and develop them before launch.

Let's take a look at the features that Uber Technologies included in their initial application and introduction to users, which led them to a successful launch. They had a total of six features: register/log-in, booking, location services, point-to-point directions, push notifications, and a price calculator. Can you believe it? Even Uber started with an MVP with a limited number of features, running a lean operation and focusing on feedback as the way forward. Through this handful of features, they were able to develop and build an early adopter community who raved about services and grew their customer base. They focused on primary features which provided users with the most value and functionality, adding the less essential ones when they had a bigger budget and proven market demand.

We conducted an interview with Aanikh Kler, co-founder and COO at Surf, to gain his perspective on how to develop products the right way.

Q: What is the best way to go about taking your MVP and building the first version of your product?

A: I feel that going from MVP to first iteration or V1 is a super important process. Usually entrepreneurs have received valuable feedback in the MVP stage and they are looking to make changes that they feel will make their offering market-ready and scalable. I feel the biggest challenge people face is getting too caught up in creating perfection or the minutiae with their V1. I am a big believer in rapid prototyping and iterating fast. Yes, you want to put out a product that is solid, but when founders get caught up in the little things, they lose valuable time when they could be getting real-world feedback and results. No one expects your product to be flawless as a young company – create strong relationships and take constructive criticism in your stride. Build a resilient and adaptable team that is designed to take feedback from users and make changes fast. There is no secret formula – different teams will be at different stages and success levels when they launch V1 – however, some will take feedback, iterate, and push to market faster until they have created a product that truly sticks.

Q: What is the best course of action to take in structuring your user or beta testing sessions?

A: In my opinion, the best course of action in early-stage testing is to try to create initial questions or areas that you as the founder would ideally like the most feedback on. Once those have been created, forget them for now, and revisit them at the end. Focus on the feedback of external users first. Put testers into buckets of different 'consumer types' and see how they distinctly interact. See what moves the needle in the different groups and find the commonalities that delight and bother all. Once you have this feedback, derive the results into tangible actions or beliefs. Then go back to your initial thoughts and see how closely they match the insights from testers. More often than not, they questioned the same things, but they came to conclusions you wouldn't have been able to reach – based on your inherent bias. The main goal in all early-stage testing is to create feedback that is purely from your target users, not the founders or internal team.

Q: Who should you approach to get involved in these user testing sessions?

A: The best people to get involved in these sessions are individuals who would fit your client profile, and individuals who are just outside your target user. Ideally, you want to bring in people who can give you feedback that will create tangible suggestions for day one; however, being able to get feedback from people partially outside the scope can lead to great insights and ideas to capture broader market share.

Q: What questions should you ask during user testing sessions?

A: There is no golden ticket to creating the best questions; many of them are case by case and depend on the area you feel you need the most feedback in. Questions pertaining to User Interface (UI), User Experience (UX), and feature sets are all different and can lead to extreme value. The main factor is to ask questions that will help lead your team to decisions and direct updates. I would say that the Net Promoter Score (NPS) question is always good. Many people will give you 'sugar-coated feedback', but asking them if they would recommend (the product) to someone else in their field often leads to more truthful answers. The more I've built product, the more I've realized how important this question is, and how powerful receiving a yes can be in creating natural customer referral networks.

From this conversation with Aanikh, it is clear that user testing sessions are paramount in developing the first version of your product in a user-oriented way. Another helpful strategy to develop your product from a user's perspective is to map out the consumer journey from start to finish.

Prioritize your MVP's features using the customer journey

Mapping out the consumer journey from beginning to end will give you an idea of what features you would like to include, and the features that you *need* to include. What are the actions the customer needs to take in order to reach the desired outcome? For example, if you're creating an application for food delivery, how many steps and inputs will the customer have to go through in order to have their meal delivered to their front door in 30 minutes? Remember, as the emphasis at this stage is still on getting to market and in front of customers *quickly*, the final iteration of your MVP will not have all the features and capabilities you plan on rolling out. We recommend going through every feature and listing the value created for the customer by completing the action. As you do so, decide on the features to prioritize by creating a list of:

- 'must-haves' (what product features are absolutely necessary to implement?)

- 'should-haves' (what features do you think the product ought to have?)

- 'could-haves' (what additional features will provide added value to customers?)

From this, it should be clear which features are adding the most value. Prioritize building the features that are absolutely necessary to move the customer forward towards their goal. In the first version of your MVP, you want to cross off all the 'must-haves'; once you're up and rolling, you can implement the 'should-have' features – those that are not essential but add to the user's experience. Then, in the final stage of your product, you can get creative and add your desired 'could-haves' – the final touches to elevate your product or service to the next level. Pay close attention to functionality when developing products, especially mobile applications, as studies show that of 3,500 users surveyed, nearly 80 per cent stated that they will only retry an app once or twice if it fails to work after the first attempt.[1]

Developing a vision

Developing a vision can be just as instrumental to the success of your company as developing a team or product. A company that has a thought-out direction for where it is aiming to go can in turn better understand what steps are required to get there. A company vision can help to inspire employees and get investors on board as well. One way to formulate a vision for your company is through the creation of a business model canvas. A business model canvas allows you to create a mind map of your business, presenting certain differences compared to the traditional business plan. It allows you to visualize your business by compartmentalizing the company into its fundamental elements. These departments include Key Partners, Key Activities, Key Resources, Value Propositions, Customer Relationships, Channels, Customer Segments, Cost Structure, and Revenue. The business model canvas provides a simple pictorial layout of each of these aspects in addition to some questions that help to guide you in determining and clarifying your vision. A business plan on the other hand is a written description of your business's strategy and concept in a way that will appeal to external investors. It is more specific in terms of what the goals of the company are, how they will be accomplished and the period of time necessary to achieve them. Another great benefit of a business model canvas is that it can show you the current holes in your business and how realistic it will be to make it profitable. If you cannot concretely think of anything to write under one of the sections (perhaps you do not have any streams of revenue yet), you know which areas of your business you need to figure out to fill such gaps.

Here is an explanation of each aspect of the business model canvas.

1 Customer segments: list the top three segments (look for segments that provide the most revenue).

2 Value proposition: how are you different from your competitors?

3 Revenue streams: list your top three revenue streams.

4 Channels: how do you communicate with your customer? How do you deliver the value proposition?

5 Customer relationships: what sorts of customer relationships are you looking to foster and how do you maintain them?

6 Key activities: what do you do every day to run your business?

7 Key resources: list the people, knowledge and money you need to run your business.

8 Key partners: list the partners that you cannot do business without (do not list suppliers).

9 Cost structure: list your top costs.

Another framework that can help you to clarify the vision for your company is what is referred to as the 'six-month road-map'. This is a short plan to define a trajectory for your business for the next six months. We recommend that you update this plan every three months (or quarter) so that your vision is aligned with the progress your company is currently making. Swish initially did it by simply taking a piece of paper and splitting the company up into definitive departments: Marketing, Finance, Human Resources, Product, Sales, and Legal. There should be two categories underneath each of these departments, *where are we right now?* and *where do we want to go?* Once you have a written-out representation of your current situation and the next destination that you want your company to reach within six months, it becomes more apparent what steps need to be taken to meet that goal.

Explaining your vision

A prime example of a founder with a stellar vision for their company from the start is notable founder Elon Musk with his company SpaceX. It can be very difficult to explain the scope of a vision for your idea in a way that anyone can understand. Try explaining the vision for a company that involves an activity as nebulous to the average person as space exploration. Musk has sought to make SpaceX a rather digestible idea for the public, as an aerospace manufacturing and space transportation services firm. Musk has said that the premise for SpaceX is to offer space exploration services at a much lower level of cost in comparison to other agencies. The goal is to one day send people to Mars, and to make space travel 'as easy as hopping on a plane'.[2] Musk highlights that SpaceX's solution is able to exist due to the advancements in aerospace engineering over the past decade, although competitors in the aerospace industry like Orbital Sciences still rely on tried and true mechanical parts from the 1960s.[3] Via a contract with NASA, SpaceX is engineering its own transportation system to 'take NASA astronauts to and from the International Space Station', after having already succeeded in sending and returning an uncrewed capsule there, showing the progress that the company is continuing to make in moving closer to its ultimate vision. What Musk has done with his vision for SpaceX aligns with a formula that all founders should aim to emulate in developing their own company visions. Musk offers a solution to performing a key activity (space travel), comparing it with something familiar to most (as easy as hopping on a plane). Then, he cites emerging trends (be it technological, economic, societal) that support the desire for this offered solution as well as milestones in recent history that have made this solution a possible reality. He presents the inspiring outcomes of SpaceX's vision (taking people to space) for seemingly little in return, after certain challenges are overcome (landing issues, bureaucratic decision making). The entire vision is summed up as an alternative to put an end to the shortcomings of the currently accepted means of operation (Musk has said that SpaceX will save US taxpayers 'at least a billion dollars' per year). This model for developing your vision[4] can help you to clarify the purpose of your company to external entities, and narrow your focus towards the actionable steps that will achieve your vision.

'How great founders present their vision': A framework[5]

1 *Our vision is that _____ [performing a key activity] will be as easy as _____ [helpful comparison].*

2 *Over the last decade, we've seen _____ [relevant trends]. These trends are set to accelerate, now that _____ [watershed technology, regulatory or competitive milestones].*

3 *Imagine if you were able to _____ [achieve inspiring outcome(s)] with just ___ [minimal user input]. We'll actually be able to deliver this as soon as we _____ [critical areas to develop in the company].*

4 *Once this is possible, our addressable market suddenly opens up from _____ [current niche customer segments] to include _____ [larger potential customer segments].*

5 *Eventually, we can eliminate _____ [injustice of the status quo]. And that's a vision we believe is worth fighting for.*

Setting expectations for your company

It is vital that you, as the founder of the business, set expectations for your business and where you want to take it. Do you have aspirations to sell the company some day? Do you eventually want to take your company public, and sell shares to public investors on the stock market? It is completely acceptable to adjust your expectations as you go along throughout the process. Your expectations will change over time and it is necessary that you make adjustments to them accordingly. Ensure that you're being practical and reflecting the nature of your business in your expectations. For example, if you're launching a food catering service in a small town of 2,000 people, it would be an unrealistic expectation to make $1 million in profit in your second year of business. That being said, you can have lofty expectations but if you begin the journey of entrepreneurship with the set goal of building a million-dollar company in the first year, you have already lost. It is crucial when setting expectations for your company that you remember that each day is about moving the needle little by little. Every successful company starts by establishing a product-market fit, then moving towards finding those 200 to 300 brand ambassadors who will actively vouch for you and your company. This is precisely what setting real expectations for your business is about. How you achieve that product-market fit and find those early supporters is supplemented by the work that is put forth on a daily basis.

Setting expectations for your business can act as a source of motivation that drives your performance. Remember that the expectations you have for your company will determine the actions that you take to meet them. This can be a driving force depending on your personality. Once you have developed a team to help build your business, however, the situation becomes more complicated because you have to be careful about the practicality of the expectations you communicate. The consequences of unreasonable expectations for your team can be demotivating good-performing employees over time. For instance, consider how a sales team that has just reached an all-time high of $10,000 in sales for the month would feel if they were immediately given the goal of $20,000 in sales for the following month. Being directed with this goal to double their recently achieved milestone could act as a source of demotivation that could potentially derail the sales team from hitting previously attainable targets again or may cause the company to plateau. Employees who had bad experiences with your unrealistic expectations in the past could lose their trust in you and will not want to return as a result. According to a Huffington Post article, 55 per cent of Generation X and Y employees would sacrifice pay for personal fulfilment in their work,[6] speaking to the fact that we are living in a world that is driven by motivation. Do not let your workforce feel demotivated, otherwise you will suffer the damaging repercussions.

In addition, the expectations that you set for your company can impact your standing with investors. You want investors to know that you're reasonable in your goals and they can be confident that given the resources, your company has the capability to meet them. There is no bluffing with investors because they know the time commitment (as well as the possible requirement to pivot the idea) that is involved in taking your company to new heights. It is best to be transparent with your expectations of your company otherwise you risk the loss of a ton of goodwill. When Surf was first pitched to investors, founders Swish and Aanikh did not convey the company as a billion-dollar social intelligence platform. Instead, they clearly communicated that the company is built by an extremely capable team with the requisite technical knowledge and entrepreneurial experience to become profitable. With this, they painted a vision for investors that would not overinflate expectations or present the company through some unfathomable lens. The lesson here is that building your business with unreasonable expectations for your team can obliterate any credibility you have as a founder, both from an employee *and* investor standpoint.

Notes

1 Shalev, K (2015) Your minimum viable product is doomed without this, *Entrepreneur*, https://www.entrepreneur.com/article/242423 (archived at https://perma.cc/672U-BDKJ)

2 Koren, M (2019) SpaceX has starry-eyed ambitions for its starship, *The Atlantic*, https://www.theatlantic.com/science/archive/2019/09/elon-musk-spacex-starship/599065/ (archived at https://perma.cc/TF96-WN3H)

3 Anderson, C (2012) Elon Musk's mission to Mars, *Wired*, https://www.wired.com/2012/10/ff-elon-musk-qa/ (archived at https://perma.cc/E3CY-FJWS)

4 Bailey, D (2019) How great founders present their vision, *Medium*, https://medium.dave-bailey.com/how-great-founders-make-their-vision-sound-inevitable-4dadb232aae7 (archived at https://perma.cc/D576-KYBS)

5 Ibid

6 Leibow, C (2014) Work/life balance for the generations, *HuffPost*, https://www.huffpost.com/entry/worklife-balance-for-the-_1_b_5992766 (archived at https://perma.cc/3NXF-FHC9)

08

Launching
and marketing
your idea

You've spent endless hours building your product, motivating your team, eating ramen, and creating a perfect vision in your mind for what launch day will look like. Trust us, there's really no way to fully prepare for the madness that happens after you launch a product or service. You're about to enter our favourite phase! Launching a product is a *big achievement*, and a true testament to all the hard work and effort you've invested to turn your idea from just another thought flowing through your head into a tangible offering in the marketplace.

Think about timing (again)

When coming up with a date to launch, be *reasonable*. You want to give yourself enough time to get your team prepped, your marketing materials ready and your backend running smoothly to handle the potential influx of clients knocking on your door. There's a lot to think about, and one of the worst mistakes entrepreneurs make is wanting to rush through this process. Take Genies, for example.

Genies is a startup based out of San Francisco and started by Akash Nigam and Evan Rosenbaum. They've built an application that will clone your personality and look, and allow your avatar to interact with the world in real time. They have raised over $23 million from some of the world's biggest celebrities, venture funds and entrepreneurs.[1] It took them three years to launch their product. They knew that if they rushed the launch, they would give away their 'secret sauce' to competitors, and not have enough leverage left to retain their users. So, we hate to rain on your parade, but your work only gets harder when thinking about launching and beyond. The good news is that now your ability to learn from your customer has exponentially gone up.

Learn from our mistakes: Surf's launch

When Surf was launching, we created all of the design assets and graphics to support PR for the product and the company; we had a great press package put together; and we had a launch date planned. We were completely ready – right? Well... by going ahead with and accepting press slightly too early, without waiting for the product to be entirely prepared, we ended up having to move back our launch date from May to June (and then to November... and then to February...). It turns out that a lot of our great PR, press and all of the great planning now had the wrong date in it, the result of happening too early.

So here's the lesson: don't rush your launch!

You should not focus on launching when the press is hot, or when you have a great story to tell, but *when your product is ready*. That (we now know!) is the number one factor when planning your full-scale launch.

How to plan for an effective launch

It is crucial that the first facet of planning for a successful launch of your product is to orient the entire team towards this objective. The launch is the new priority for all members of the team, and this means that we have all hands on deck in planning for the launch. Designate distinct roles to each person – one person can be assigned to the role of facilitating and organizing the operational aspects of the launch. This responsibility includes booking a venue and having a set agenda for what will occur at the product launch (and seeing through that it gets done).

There is a lot of logistical work that needs to occur on launch day, and this is an important role that warrants particular attention to detail. There should also be one team member with the responsibility of ensuring that the product does not malfunction on the day of the launch. Especially for an early company, you cannot afford to lose credibility with external entities, and having your product malfunction is a guaranteed way to cause this distrust. In the stress of launch day, it is easy to get lost in the minute details of the launch and consequently have avoidable things go wrong. Planning for mishaps like a malfunction in the product is a key way to relieve some of the pressure of the day, as you can have the peace of mind that one of your team members has fulfilled their task of having a fully functioning product ready for demonstration.

Another responsibility that can be designated to a particular member of your team is to create and distribute any marketing materials that will help to raise awareness for your launch. This responsibility can consist of sending out a press release to media personnel, or creating informational graphics that can be used for distribution on the streets or on social media platforms (more on marketing strategies later). Remember that although one member of the team may be tasked with the marketing materials for your launch, it should be the responsibility of the entire team to circulate and share the message of your launch, in any way that they can (posting on their individual social media, telling friends and family about the launch).

What separates the good from the bad?

Now that you have laid out a meticulous operational structure for your launch, you may still be wondering: what separates a successful launch from one that has failed? To do this, it is helpful to examine both good and bad notable product launches of the past.

The good

A stellar example of a product launch that was an immediate hit with customers is something you have likely interacted with before: a Rubik's Cube. The toy burst onto the international scene in 1980 and was instantly adored by puzzle-solving enthusiasts of all ages, with 100 million cubes sold by 1982.[2] The cube, which was initially intended for architectural design students, has become the best-selling toy in

history, with a booming secondary market of products form-
ing from its global popularity (cube-solving competitions,
list-topping guidebooks on cube-solving strategies etc).
According to the cube's inventor, Erno Rubik, the product
became such a phenomenon due to society's 'basic desire to
create order out of chaos' and its innate inclination to 'basic
contradictions: simplicity and complexity, dynamism and
stability, pleasure and frustration…'. Product founders know
there is more to it than that. The product was completely
novel to the toy market at the time, where dolls and trucks
reigned supreme. The Rubik's Cube was a puzzle that everyone wanted to try out for themselves to experience the challenge first-hand. Once you pick up the cube, you simply
cannot stop at one attempt; it is precisely this entrancement
among customers that allowed Rubik's cube to be ubiqui-
tous. The lesson to take from this is that you want your audience to view your product as one that they will return to
again and *again*, occupying them completely as they interact
with your product. It is worth communicating this aspect to
customers during your launch (potentially via a demonstration, various walkthrough use cases) and once this objective
is achieved, this is a direct indication that your product
launch has served its purpose.

The bad

Often, even the most well-intentioned product launches fail
to reach the ambitious expectations that they were set out to
meet. Such was the case for carbonated drink giant Coca-
Cola when they unveiled *Coca Cola C2* in 2004. This iteration of the drink was intended specifically for males between
the ages of 20 and 40. Market research conducted by the
company discovered that males in this age range enjoyed the

taste of regular Coke, but not the calories and carbs that they consumed from it, whereas they found the appeal in the zero-calorie Diet Coke, but were drawn away by the overall taste and belief that it was 'feminine'.[3] The C2 was introduced to provide a compromise for the flaws in its current offerings, and the company demonstrated its confidence in the idea by allocating a $50 million advertising budget behind it. Just three years later, the product was discontinued. As it turned out, men were not satisfied with a low-calorie rendition of Coke, and the market trend against carbs diminished quickly over time.[4] Even worse, the C2 edition had the negative effect of *cannibalizing* the sales of the company's other offerings (eating away at the sales of other product lines), holding total growth stagnant in the North American market. As we have discussed in previous chapters, MVP testing is essential before launching your product. So why did Coca-Cola not see these shortcomings before committing to launch? In essence, the company was not specific enough during its user testing sessions and did not determine whether a valid level of demand existed before investing into this new offering. Coca-Cola had conflated feedback received from multiple product lines, which led to an inadequate understanding of the product that the core demographic truly desired. Even the largest companies in the world can make mistakes when asking questions during user testing sessions. The lesson for founders is that when considering your product launch, ensure that you have definitive and concrete differences between what your product offers and what is currently available in the industry (make sure to *communicate* these differences during your launch). In addition, ask yourself if your solution is for a problem that will persist for several years, or if instead it's an answer for a temporary fad in society today. If your product fits the latter category, you can still have a profitable product on your hands but reconsider how much you're investing into the product financially.

The ugly

From these two opposing product launches, it is common to assume that all successful launches can be gauged by how well the release translates to customer orders or new customer engagement, after the launch has taken place. However, an often-overlooked point to consider about any product launch is how the company is able to react to spontaneously rapid growth. If your product garners the immediate adoption you have dreamed of, do you have the requisite manpower and resources to support this newfound influx in demand? In the wake of the deadly West Nile virus epidemic, American Biophysics Corporation launched the *Mosquito Magnet*, which uses carbon dioxide gas to lure and trap mosquitoes. Not long after, the product became a top seller at Home Depot and other retailers, leading the company to make the decision to expand its manufacturing operation from Rhode Island to a plant in China.[5] A consequence of this decision was that the quality of the product deteriorated, driving away customers and resulting in a severe devaluation of the company. What was once a firm that amassed $70 million in yearly revenues eventually sold for a mere $6 million in an acquisition. Founders who have lofty ambitions of unprecedented growth for their company in a short period of time must be prepared with a plan if this ultimately becomes a reality upon launch. Be careful what you wish for because uncontrollable growth can have fatal consequences for any startup.

Marketing your launch

When it comes down to it, no matter how much you plan for the execution of your launch, you will not make a true splash in the market if nobody knows about it. In developing an actionable strategy for your launch, you will see a substantial difference in engagement when directing your focus toward people, rather than the product. What does this mean? A founder who did an incredible job illustrating this concept was the late Steve Jobs. Commanding the attention of the audience during Apple product launches in his signature black turtleneck and New Balance sneakers, Jobs consistently made it his mission to put the people who were going to buy the product before the product itself. When promoting products, he made it a priority to mention how the product will affect you, the end consumer, before elaborating about product technological specifications that would enable the user to harness some benefit (eg the iPhone condensing into an all-in-one phone and music player). How will this product bring the user value and meet a need that they may not have known they had until now? You want to delve deeper into the experience the user will enjoy when interacting with your product. The core of this strategy is embedded in how the product will impact the life of the consumer for the better, satisfying one of their distinct pain points. Use technological aspects as the bridge that will get the user to the desirable new normal that you're painting in the mind of the intended audience.

Another great marketing tactic that has been adopted by many companies to spread the word about a company's product launch is creating and distributing a **press release**.

Provide a concise elevator pitch about your product launch that you can send out to respected journalists, bloggers and micro-influencers who have the platform to reach your target audience. Your press release should ideally be sent out two weeks prior to your launch date. As per a study by Fractl, journalists working at reputable media firms get upwards of 70 email pitches on a daily basis.[6] On a practical level, there is a very slim chance that they will see even a tenth of the press releases received, and so it becomes increasingly crucial that you give yourself a fighting chance to be acknowledged amid the fierce competition.

How to write a captivating press release

What does an effective and complete press release consist of? A great press release must aim to meet the following criteria: be gripping from beginning to end, relevant to the selected audience, and concise in length (no more than a page). Going further, in order to satisfy these conditions, consider the gradual structure of any strong press release. They all begin with a short headline that plays to the intrigue of the intended reader of the piece. A simple subject line with the use of descriptive verbs and clear language can go a long way in setting the foundation for a worthy press release. To illustrate this point, consider these two article headlines which both discuss formal email etiquette. The first is: *An adequate method of emailing someone in a formal manner.* Compare this headline to the following: *Do you make these formal emailing mistakes?* In addition to containing fewer words and using simpler language, the latter example is able to grip the reader by prompting them to visualize themselves making such errors in email etiquette, probing them to discover whether or not they do. Translate this strategy over to the context of your product and you can entice journalists to give your press release a read through.

After that, you want to make sure that you're getting straight to the point within the first paragraph of your press release. Remember that you do not want your press release to extend beyond a page in length, and journalists are typically short on time while reading these pieces as it is. Include the Who, What, Where, When, Why and How of your product launch within this introductory paragraph so that the journalist has an immediate gauge of how well your company aligns with their available audience. Saving them from having to search throughout your press release for information can have a favourable influence on their decision to send out your release.

To provide credibility to your product launch and company in general, it is worth including a quote or two from esteemed stakeholders in your company. This could be an investor, an early adopter, or even a member of your core team who will provide a statement about the crux of the product launch announcement. Rather than a surface-level explanation of the product launch, the quotes used should showcase how the launch will have a pertinent impact in disrupting the industry, the general ecosystem, and most importantly, in serving value for the customer. In the next paragraph, you can opt to add in a few relevant background details that you think would resonate with the intended audience most. This could be anything from the thought process behind the development of your product, to the perceived future outlook that the company is working towards. Be cautious that you're not overinflating this section with a load of unnecessary detail. Stick to the purpose of your press release: building attention for your launch. If there is a detail about your brand and its conception that can supplement the narrative you're conveying, the second to last paragraph would be the perfect location. Finally, conclude your press release by adding what is known as a 'boilerplate'. At the end of every press release, this section highlights what exactly your company is in the business of doing, its approximate size (employees), location of headquarters, as well as any social media platforms that the audience can follow to keep updated. No press release is truly complete without the inclusion of a boilerplate.

It is imperative that each team member has a copy of your press release so that everyone is on the same page for launch day. In addition, each member of the team can play a part in spreading the press release to individuals they believe will be appropriate. Your product launch can even be thought of as an event. Each member of the company can be responsible for inviting a particular set of community leaders, journalists, family, potential customers or investors to this event and launching your product in this fashion.

Creating content to promote your launch

Another aspect of marketing your product launch is the graphics and videos that you put out into the world. The most pertinent question that you should be asking yourself in regard to your marketing content: is it shareable among customers and members of your team? When your promotional videos and graphics can be conveyed to others without any direct interference on your behalf, your message can be diffused organically with less effort.

A great way to build hype around your product before launch day is to create a snippet of your product in use, and share this video clip across multiple platforms. This is ideally done two weeks beforehand, and can prepare potential customers for what they can expect for launch day. To illustrate the value of this method, think of any popular video game that has come out in the past two decades. The most anticipated video games generate buzz through the virality of a gameplay trailer which compels potential customers, inching them closer towards deciding to give the game a try once the opportunity arises. The beauty of creating a video trailer of your product in action is that the product does not need to be a video game in order for a 'gameplay trailer' to be effective. As long as your audience understands what your product does and what it is used for, you can be confident that this 'product trailer' has served its core purpose.

Boundaries and balance

Before launching, please realize that as entrepreneurs, we spend so much time creating our businesses that they can start to feel a part of our identity. With all the energy, perseverance, inspiration and love we pour into its creation, it is very easy to become attached and fixated on the company's success – especially after launch –and use it to validate our own sense of self-worth. Don't make this mistake! *It is extremely important* that you make the distinction between yourself and your business now, as a failure to do so can lead to unnecessary suffering. Creating this boundary successfully can not only help protect your own well-being, but it can actually lead to better business: an entrepreneur whose self-identity is separate and distinct from their business can take their ego out of the picture, and actually take well-intentioned criticism in a constructive manner, using the feedback to improve their business. Besides, as Airbnb founder and CEO Brian Chesky puts it, 'If you launch and no one notices, launch again. We launched three times'.[7] In reality, there is truly no limit to the amount of times that you're allowed to launch your product, granted that with each new launch you're bringing a modified, enhanced version to the market.

Notes

1 Constine, J (2018) Genies brings lifelike avatars to other apps with $10M from celebrities, *TechCrunch*, https://techcrunch.com/2018/11/19/genies-avatars/ (archived at https://perma.cc/XT77-9JHX)

2 Nagraj, N (2016) Solving Rubik's Cube is the least interesting thing about the puzzle, *New York Post*, https://nypost.com/2016/10/31/how-the-internet-brought-the-rubiks-cube-back-to-life/ (archived at https://perma.cc/A44J-9YZP)

3 Schneider, J and Hall, J (2014) Why most product launches fail, *Harvard Business Review*, https://hbr.org/2011/04/why-most-product-launches-fail (archived at https://perma.cc/SZR8-X7XQ)

4 Ibid

5 Ibid

6 Fractl (2019) Here's what not to do to get your content featured on major online publishers, www.frac.tl/work/marketing-research/pitching-pet-peeves (archived at https://perma.cc/8R6W-BFYW)

7 Aydin, R (2019) How 3 guys turned renting air mattresses in their apartment into a $31 billion company, Airbnb, *Business Insider*, https://www.businessinsider.com/how-airbnb-was-founded-a-visual-history-2016-2 (archived at https://perma.cc/8R6W-BFYW)

09
Fostering collaboration

Now more than ever, companies from startups to Fortune 500s are trying to figure out how to create an environment where people feel inspired, respected and capable of working effectively with others. We've thought a lot about this over the last few years of building our own companies.

When Swish set out to hire his early employees for Surf, he didn't realize that many outstanding candidates preferred working remotely over working in the office, particularly in an expensive city like Toronto with its record high rent prices. It makes sense though; workplaces have evolved dramatically in the last decade. Open concept offices and satellite offices are common and have been shown to boost employee satisfaction when the alternative is a long commute. Currently, nearly half of Surf's employees work remotely, and they make up the majority of the marketing and product development teams.

Surf allows their employees to work remotely because they don't believe creativity comes from being in the same place all the time. They prefer to encourage their employees to work out of places that inspire them to work harder and feel better. That being said, the need for clear communication and effective management is even higher with remote teams.

Effective team management results in collaboration and collaboration challenges employees to think bigger and get things done more quickly. It will allow your team to improve on their weaknesses by working with others that have mastered a specific skill.

Five tips on fostering better team collaboration and culture

Keep everyone in the know (from the beginning)

When you hire remote employees, just like non-remote employees, it's important to set expectations for them immediately. Let your team know how many times a week you want to talk with them, what sort of results you're looking for and what you have seen work in the past. Once you give your team a task, make sure to stay up to date on their progress. The Computing Technology Industry Association said that 28 per cent of first-year employees reported that poor communication was the primary reason for failing to deliver a project within its original time frame.[1]

Using apps like Asana or Notion is a great way to track your team's progress on a task and give them feedback instantly. This is especially important for CEOs as they need to be able to gauge which employees (including remote employees) are performing to their potential and which ones are not. Tracking their work in real time, whether it's the company's budget or our marketing strategy, is a great way for you or your project managers to keep them accountable.

At Surf, Swish uses technology to connect new employees to existing employees who have been at the company for longer. He encourages all employees to instant message each other over Slack, as an alternative to email, when they start working at Surf. As a result, Swish feels like his employees have an easier time asking for help and making important team decisions more quickly.

Regardless of whether your team is working remotely or in an office, it's also important to keep them in the know throughout the week. Swish makes sure to have weekly online meetings, and he always sends the agenda with the invite so it's clear what his team will be going over. It helps his employees prepare for the meeting in advance and compile any questions they have around the discussion areas.

Be accessible (as much as you can)

Your company's culture is the combination of the expectations you set, and the behaviours you embody as a leader. When it comes to communication, the culture you build around collaboration will come first from your own responsiveness, and patterns of collaboration with your own team – your actions will set the norms and behaviours of those around you, who will in turn influence those around them. The technological leap we as a society have gone through to get to this point is something we never take for granted. It's made running a business and collaborating with our teams much more accessible.

At Surf, every week, they have a team huddle, three team calls, a Paranoia Session (which we'll talk about later in this chapter) and a check-in with every employee (even if they are remote). Swish doesn't believe that too much communication is something to be feared. Instead it is something to be encouraged as more communication provides your employees with more chances to become closer to each other and eventually work better with each other.

Engage regularly and efficiently

About a year ago, Swish was invited by Brian Scudamore (CEO, 1800-GOT-JUNK) to visit their head office in Vancouver. At the office, he saw their morning huddle. It was a high-energy session but what Swish truly loved about it was how inclusive it was. The Vancouver office teleconferenced the Toronto team into the meeting and also allowed the Toronto team to share their screen so they could share their successes over the last week. This was how Swish came up with the idea to have a team huddle at Surf via weekly online meetings with our remote and non-remote teams. It's built excitement and camaraderie between employees that don't have daily face-to-face communication. It's also been a great way for our remote teams to feel part of a bigger operation.

Whenever you can, especially on events that bring the whole team together, try to loop in your remote teams virtually. In today's world, there's no excuse not to do this.

Have reliable tools

The number one way Swish has been able to create a collaborative environment at Surf is by investing in proper tools. Before he made his first hire, he went online and made sure to purchase software that would allow our employees, especially those that are remote, to have the best experience possible. Why? Because especially for young employees coming into the workplace, building a tech-enabled environment is a must. In 2016, Blue Source found that 81 per cent of millennials thought that 'state-of-the-art technology' is more important to an ideal working environment than perks or amenities.[2]

Swish wanted to make sure that his employees could download files easily, schedule meetings with others quickly, and feel truly immersed in conference calls. Giving your employees better tools will help them be more productive.

Many of the tools needed to enhance communication are not costly but even if they were, consider them as an investment in your company's future. The same 2016 Blue Source study found that productivity improves by up to 25 per cent in organizations with connected employees.[3]

Get to know your team (past their resume)

Swish prides himself on really trying to get to know his team throughout the process of working with them. It's a challenging endeavour given how fast we've grown and how busy our employees are. That's why at Surf, he created a weekly session called the Paranoia Session. In it, he had every employee sit around our boardroom or teleconference in. Swish encouraged them to tell him what worries them the most. Most of the conversations are around where the business is going or specific experiences on the product or sales side. What Swish noticed is that sharing vulnerabilities and doubts in an honest way has led to some of Surf's best ideas being brought forward. He also noticed that his employees are becoming more confident about speaking up and sharing their honest opinions.

Notes

1 Rosencrance, L (2007) Survey: Poor communication causes most IT project failures, *Computerworld*, https://www. computerworld.com/article/2543770/survey--poor-communication-causes-most-it-project-failures.html (archived at https://perma.cc/J3G4-BEY5)

2 White, SK (2016) Millennials are shaking up workplace communication, *CIO*, https://www.cio.com/article/3082775/millennials-are-shaking-up-workplace-communication.html (archived at https://perma.cc/Y33H-8WPA)

3 Nicholson, M (2020) Work flexibility is boosting productivity for growing businesses, *Home Business*, https://homebusinessmag.com/management/working-smarter/work-flexibility-boosting-productivity-growing-businesses/ (archived at https://perma.cc/AAN7-4PY6)

10

Understanding traction: developing business metrics

As you grow your business, you'll find that in many meetings with potential investors, the question of 'traction' will come up frequently. What does 'traction' mean? Traction is the extent to which an idea or product gains popularity and acceptance, and can be measured by things like purchases, subscriptions, clicks, views, likes, etc. In essence, investors are looking for proof that you've built something that people want. Easier said than done.

Understanding what sort of metrics you need to generate and measure is crucial to identifying strengths and weaknesses in your business. Traction, for example, is also one of the most significant indicators of your future potential for later-stage investors. This chapter will evaluate the most significant metrics all businesses should concern themselves with when it comes to understanding traction, and the sorts of specific metrics different business types should focus on, depending on their business model. The sort of traction you're looking for will depend on the stage your venture is at. We will discuss pre- and post-revenue traction indicators here.

Pre-revenue traction

Generally, people consider traction and paying customers to be synonymous. So, for a pre-revenue company, what does traction look like? First and foremost, you want to establish that you are solving a problem people will pay for – getting potential customers to give testimonials and letters of intent is a clear demonstration of this. If you have identified a problem, a target market, and conducted your market research, gathering early traction should be easy (which it almost never is).

In the process of reaching out to people or organizations in your target market and working to better understand their pain points, you are presented with the perfect opportunity to ask them what they think about your potential solution. If they do not like your solution it is always worth asking them why, and more importantly, focusing on learning more about their specific problem rather than the various features they propose for your solution. As you iterate your solution, you'll encounter more and more potential customers who express their support for your product or service. As you near a proposed product or service that merits moving forward with, begin asking potential customers if they would provide a written statement expressing their willingness to purchase your solution once launched. These written statements need not be contractually binding, though if your potential customers are willing to sign a formal letter of agreement, this is all the better for your business.

At Autumn, we chose three key metrics to evaluate our progress. The first was the number of new users we attracted, the second was the number of words per user analysed by our artificial intelligence (AI), and the third was the number of returning users. The first and third are fairly intuitive; they give us and our investors a sense of how quickly we are growing, and the extent to which we are able to deliver on our value proposition to those users. The second metric is somewhat more specific to the business model Autumn relies on. At the core of our business is an AI model that allows users to predict how their psychological well-being will fluctuate in the future given the text data they generate – it turns out your language is an incredibly accurate and early indicator of how you feel now, and how you will feel in the future. In order to improve the accuracy of this AI model, it needs to be trained, and it *is* trained on language data – the more language data the more accurate it becomes. Measuring the amount of language users authorize the algorithm to analyse tells us both how much users trust our platform and how much training data we have (we put full control of data and data analyses in the hands of the individual, which means they are the only ones that see the results, but it still takes time for users to become comfortable enough to authorize access to certain data sources like email).

Post-revenue traction

It is crucial to establish a frame of reference for understanding post-revenue traction metrics. Any metric your venture generates will only provide insight if compared to something, be it an industry average, historical data, or past projections. More often than not, it is the trends in a given traction metric that generate real interest more than any number in and of itself.

The three traction metrics we will look into are customer retention, churn, and duration. These will be used to assess your customer lifetime value, a crucial piece of information that allows you to build your financial predictions. *Customer Retention Rate* (CRR) is calculated based on three variables: the number of customers at the end of a given time period (E); the number of new customers acquired during that given time period (N); and the number of customers at the start of the given time period (S). The formula for CRR is:

$$CRR = ((E-N)/S) \times 100$$

Why is it important? Customer retention is up to 7X less costly than customer acquisition on average, and the likelihood of converting an existing customer into a repeat customer is 60–70 per cent. Essentially, it is easier to keep customers than it is to find new ones, and CRR helps you measure that. Indeed, depending on the business and your customer lifetime value, a 5 per cent increase in CRR could generate 25 to 95 per cent increase in profits, according to recent studies.

Customer Churn Rate is the rate at which customers stop buying from your company during a given time period. In order to calculate your churn rate (CR) you will need to know the number of customers lost during the given time period (L); the number of new customers acquired during that time period (A); and the number of customers at the start of a given time period (S). The formula for CR is:

$$CR = ((L-A)/S) \times 100$$

A positive churn indicates your company has a net loss of customers; a negative churn rate indicates your company has a net gain of customers. For example, if a company has 100 customers at the beginning of the month (S), acquires seven new customers that month (A) and loses 10 customers (L), then the company has a churn rate of:

$$((10-7)/100) \times 100 = 3\%$$

Meaning that the company in question loses 3 per cent of its customer base over the given time period of one month. Ideally, a company has a negative churn rate, or in other words an expanding customer base.

Customer Duration, also called customer lifetime, is calculated by taking the reciprocal of churn rate (1/churn rate). If we take the company above, their average customer lifetime is 1/3 per cent churn per month or 1/0.03 churn per month = 33 months. This value is then used to provide you with your customer lifetime value.

Customer Lifetime Value (CLV or LTV) is a prediction of all the value a customer will provide a business over the course of their relationship with that business. Customer lifetime value requires that you know the average value of a sale, the average number of repeat transactions per customer per average customer lifetime, and the initial cost of customer acquisition. It is worth noting that CLV and churn rate are hard to quantify in the early stages of a company. You need to have accumulated at least one year of sales data to be able to make concrete assumptions on these indicators. The simple formula for calculating customer lifetime value is:

CLV = (average annual profit contribution per customer) x (number of years an average customer remains) – (initial cost of customer acquisition)

The slightly more complex formula for calculating customer lifetime value includes calculating the discounted future value of a customer for each year after the customer acquisition event, or:

CLV = ((average annual profit contribution per customer) x (cumulative customer retention rate) – (initial cost of customer acquisition)) x (appropriate future discount rate for each year under consideration)

For example, if we were to calculate the lifetime value of a video streaming subscriber who spends $10 every month for four years, their CLV using the simple formula would be:

($10 x 12 months) x 4 years = $480 in lifetime revenue

Customer Acquisition Cost (CAC) is the last (and perhaps most simple) metric we will discuss, and while not directly related to measuring traction, it is important for calculating your customer lifetime value, and things such as marketing spend and profitability. To calculate your customer acquisition cost, divide the total amount spent on acquiring new customers by the number of customers acquired within the period of time the money was spent. Now this can become more complicated depending on the variety of marketing channels used and your ability to attribute certain marketing efforts to new customers. For example, a car dealership calculating their customer acquisition cost might include the salary of a showroom car salesperson, the cost of ads in the newspaper, television ads, social media ads, website hosting fees, etc. Under ideal conditions, your business will have perfect data, allowing for the quick and easy calculation of customer acquisitions per marketing channel. This is rarely the case, however, outside of click-through digital marketing where you are able to more readily identify how many people view an advert and subsequently purchase your solution. Consequently, as your business grows it will be important to do research to determine the effectiveness of different marketing channels such that you can optimize your return on investment. In the short term it means a lot of guesswork and iteratively improving those assumptions as you collect more data over time. But remember, a good product can go a long way towards reducing customer acquisition costs – building something that sells itself is always preferable compared to investing heavily in marketing.

In order for your business to achieve sustainable growth, your customer lifetime value should be approximately *three times* your customer acquisition cost, and customer acquisition costs should be recovered within 12 months after customer acquisition for subscription businesses. Market leaders among businesses that generate recurring revenue from customers have a customer lifetime value closer to five times customer acquisition costs. But beyond the metrics, building something truly valuable for people is a fundamentally iterative process. All too often, we become so obsessed with metrics that we forget what we are measuring in the first place. Peter Drucker, the famed business thinker, once said, 'There is nothing so useless as doing efficiently that which should not be done at all'.[1] And as is frequently the case when relying on traction or financial metrics to diagnose the fundamental health of your business, it is crucial not to lose sight of the things that will improve traction more fundamentally – focus on building something people really want.

As is discussed further in Chapter 13 on scaling, the best way to gather traction is to do things that do not scale – go out of your way to truly understand and address the needs of your customers.

Note

1 Drucker, P (1963) Managing for business effectiveness, *Harvard Business Review*, https://hbr.org/1963/05/managing-for-business-effectiveness (archived at https://perma.cc/WEX7-9UAF).

11
Fundraising strategies

Swish sees his role as CEO of Surf as encompassing four key responsibilities: setting a vision for the company, fundraising, hiring, and high-level sales. Out of these four responsibilities, he finds fundraising to be the hardest. It's not only because getting people and institutions to fund you is challenging, but also that while you're fundraising, it's difficult to focus on any other aspects of the business. Many entrepreneurs never really spend time on their business since they are constantly on the road fundraising. This chapter will go over how to think about fundraising and strategies to make your pitch better. The next chapter will go over fundraising necessities including having your financials in order and figuring out a proper valuation for your company.

Before getting into any strategies, it's worth noting that we do not believe every entrepreneur should fundraise. Now more than ever it's become easier to 'bootstrap' a business to profitability. Bootstrapping a business means that rather than fundraising, the business grows off of the revenue it generates. You can do this by working a full-time job and reinvesting your salary into the business, or through some alternative way that does not involve giving up ownership of your company. It is much better to sell a company valued at X when you own 100 per cent of it vs 40 per cent of it. That said, there *are* reasons to fundraise. Firstly, fundraising helps offset early startup costs (developing your product, paying early employees, etc). Secondly, it can be useful in the growth stage of your company, especially when you figure out which growth strategies are working well. If you realize that for every $1 you spend on Facebook ads you're making $4, you might want to double down on buying more ads. To cover those costs and to move quickly, fundraising can be helpful.

Swish has raised more than US$4 million for his business Surf. What he realized is that most investors, especially VCs, tend to invest in ideas they think will reach a billion-dollar valuation quickly. They invest in areas that are incredibly disruptive and rapidly changing (eg quantum computing, blockchain, AI, etc). Swish's co-founder Aanikh always said that most VCs are more likely to invest in a company that has a 25 per cent chance of becoming a unicorn than a company that has a 75 per cent chance of being a $100 million company. That was a hard bullet for Swish to swallow since he knew he was tackling a billion-dollar market but up until recently, he had no idea what his billion-dollar vision was. Moreover, Swish thought it would take him two weeks to raise his initial round of $500,000. It took him more than three months. Part of the reason it took this long could be because he raised funds during the summer, which is a difficult time of the year to get hold of people. More importantly, he also came into the fundraising process not well prepared enough from a materials standpoint. He didn't have any financial projections ready, and before the process started, he didn't even have a completed pitch deck to use. He was relying solely on a one-pager he had drafted and his dashing good looks.

As you undergo fundraising rounds, the process gets easier but raising that first big round is always tough.

Tips on fundraising

Make money from day one

This was a belief Michael Hyatt (entrepreneur and investor) conveyed to Swish early on. He once texted Swish, 'revenue cures all evils'. While the product was being developed, Swish and his team at Surf looked at as many ways to make money from day one as possible. They did some consulting work for brands. Surf ran a merchandise service for influencers while also providing their own merchandise and sponsoring events like the NBA Summer League. What was the most effective for not only sales but for business development, was Surf's data reports. The algorithm they had constructed was active months before the beta came out. They could churn data and put a user's most engaged and influential fans into a CSV file that they could then upload to Twitter, Instagram or Facebook to run retargeting campaigns. One of Surf's successful case studies here was Western Union. They signed a lucrative $25,000 deal with them to provide advice on LinkedIn and data reports for three months.

Find your lead investor early

Your lead investor does not have to be in tech. So much investing comes down to how a potential investor assesses risk. If you already have a lead investor on board, it can help other investors feel confident in your project. If you are currently fundraising, read Startup North's 'One Post to Rule Them All'. Albeit the list is from 2015, it's still a great article online summarizing some major investors.[1] Try reaching out to them on LinkedIn or Instagram!

Set a deadline and stick to it

Swish didn't do this, and he really wishes he did. When investors asked Swish 'I'm busy, when is the round open until?', he rarely ever replied with a firm deadline. When you think of your fundraising process, create three goals: a number you need to hit to keep a healthy runway (how many months your company will stay alive for), a number you would like to hit, and a number that is in your dreams. Make sure to provide deadlines for each – the closest deadline for the number you need to hit to stay afloat. Tell your investors that so they feel like they need to get a move on and pay attention to the deal.

Put some money in yourself (if possible)

Investing your own money into your company shows investors that you have skin in the game. That is what Swish, his co-founder Aanikh, and his CFO Trevor did.

Be tenacious and persistent

Follow up, provide value to people you want to get on board, and be resilient when you hear the word 'no'. See every no as an opportunity to get feedback. If you want someone to give feedback, be shameless and ask them for help. Swish has found that most people don't grow personally because they don't ask for help. Swish does (sometimes too much), and it has helped him learn things a lot faster.

Don't think that you have to raise from one or two people

In Surf's second round, they brought on 14 angel investors. Some might say that is too many and that it clutters your cap table (list of your investors) but Swish begs to differ. When you are conducting an angel round, it doesn't matter how many people you bring on as long as you think that each person can strategically help the business beyond money (eg advice, expertise, connections, partnerships, etc). Also, the benefit of having more people on your cap table is that when you go to fundraise again, you will have more people (and their networks) to tap for additional funds.

Stay lean

On a flight to Santiago, Chile, Swish read Reid Hoffman's *Blitzscaling*, a book that Reid believed served as the blueprint for a billion-dollar company. Not only was the book really insightful, but it motivated Swish to commit fully to Surf and to stay lean. Reid noticed that many startups run out of money because after raising a round their founders and key employees take high salaries hoping that they will be able to raise another round quickly.[2] Swish didn't want to operate that way with Surf, especially in the early days when Surf was not generating as much revenue. Your investors will love you for that mentality.

Manage your investors properly

Your investors don't want to hear from you every day, but they *do* want to be kept in the loop on the major things that are affecting the company, and how they can provide support. Swish sends out a monthly investor update to all of Surf's investors and advisors. This has a breakdown of all the great things that happened in the month, the areas the team has grown in, and the challenges they are facing.

So you have been given all these tips and you feel ready to present your idea to an investor. How do you go about pitching and convincing an investor to fund your idea? Venture capitalists are notorious for being selective. The rule of thumb for them is that for every 1,000 pitches they hear, they only fund about 100 of them. The way to increase your chances of securing a cheque from them is by building an irresistible and unforgettable pitch.

Tips on pitching

Have a good slide deck

Swish has been an entrepreneur and has also had experience in venture capital. As an associate at JB Fitzgerald, he saw hundreds of pitches a week. He noticed that most people didn't spend time making their deck look good, or having a professional designer come in and make slides look polished. We advise that you spend some extra money and time to make your deck visually appealing. There are times you will be pitching in person but there are also other instances where you might be doing your pitch over the phone and what an investor will be mainly looking at is your deck. If you're interested in seeing some good decks, check out Y Combinator's blog on pitch decks.[3] If you need someone reliable to design your deck, feel free to reach out to one of Surf's investors, Jake Ratner (@ratnercreative on Instagram). He has designed many decks, and is always looking to work with great entrepreneurs.

Show enthusiasm

You don't need to be the most extroverted person in the world to deliver a solid pitch. That being said, you definitely don't want to be quiet, shy and nervous when delivering it either. You want to show your passion for your industry or solution. That could come in the form of providing extra information in select areas to show investors you are an expert in the field, or by remaining confident when investors are asking questions.

Keep a good pace

It's important to keep a good pace when delivering your pitch. Make sure to especially go slow and be clear when explaining your problem statement and solution: these two parts are by far the most important in any pitch. If an investor has to ask you after your presentation, 'What problem are you solving?' or 'So if I understand your solution correctly…?' you are likely not going to be walking out of the room with a deal.

Always do your best to state numbers

Investors love hearing numbers, whether it's about your market size, your revenue to date or the value of any potential deals you are aiming to score in the future. Put things in perspective for your investor, don't let them assume what a 'big' or 'small' deal looks like.

Be honest

This might be the most important tip. Quinn and Swish have been in board meetings where entrepreneurs have flat out lied about their competition or about what their product can do. There is a difference between selling your vision and selling lies. The best entrepreneurs are the ones that can be reasonable and provide nuance to their answers. For example, instead of hoping that the person in front of you doesn't bring up a competitor, name two or three (even if they are indirect) so that your investor knows that you have a stronger awareness of your market.

Explain how the investor makes their money back

One of Swish's mentors, Michael Hyatt (former Chairman, BlueCat Networks), always told Swish, 'You need to follow the cheque'. What he meant by that was that you need to explain to an investor very clearly how the money that leaves their pocket multiplies over time, and comes back to them in a greater sum. This could be in the form of an acquisition, IPO, expansion, or another scenario. Paint a picture that is in alignment with your vision and provide points on what the timeline looks like and why that timeline is going to play out the way you want.

Solely relying on your pitch is a recipe for disaster. Even if you deliver the greatest pitch of all time, an investor might say no on the basis of not being interested in your industry, not believing that your solution will work, or deeming your traction to be premature. So while you focus on making a good pitch, understand that a great pitch for a bad business is not as favourable as having a poor pitch for a good business.

Notes

1 Crow, D (2015) One post to rule them all, *StartupNorth*, http://startupnorth.ca/2014/06/24/one-post-to-rule-them-all/ (archived at https://perma.cc/GL8U-CMQF)

2 Yeh, C and Hoffman, R (2018) *Blitzscaling: The lightning-fast path to building massively valuable companies*, Currency

3 Hale, K (2021) How to design a better pitch deck, *Y Combinator*, https://www.ycombinator.com/library/4T-how-to-design-a-better-pitch-deck (archived at https://perma.cc/BCQ5-MT23)

12
Fundraising necessities

Entire books have been written on fundraising, and yet it often remains more of an art than a science. What we'll cover here will provide you with the necessary information to begin planning and positioning yourself and your venture to maximize the chances of investment, if necessary, for the growth of your company.

The financials of fundraising

Before we get into the specifics of fundraising, investors or valuation, we'll start with the exceptionally exciting and riveting topic of financials. Everyone loves them. Or rather, everyone loves to hate them. But they're really important. Having a solid grasp of the basics will provide you with a strong competitive advantage, and will teach you all the things you don't normally learn in school. Our recommendation is to build out your personal finances in a similar manner – financial planning never hurt anyone and will set you up for a secure financial future.

Weak financial literacy is one of the leading causes of small business failure, and entrepreneurs are no different. 'Entrepreneurs aren't the only business leaders who don't understand finance'.[1] While not the most glamorous aspect of building and running a business, your business finances are pivotal for a strong startup. The maths behind a startup's financials is not complicated. First you must know the difference between your financial statements and your financial projections. Financial *statements* are written records that allow you to diagnose your financial strengths and weaknesses, and determine the sustainability and profitability of your venture; they capture and reflect information that has already taken place. Financial *projections* are estimates of your venture's future performance built on a number of assumptions, including future revenues, expenses and financing. Financial projections are assumptions and estimates of your venture's future performance which don't reflect current or past information. The more historical data you have (financial statements), the more realistic and accurate your financial projections will become as your assumptions are honed through analysis of real data and venture performance.

There are three core applications of your financials: feasibility analysis, fundraising and management. Financial projections are particularly important in feasibility analysis and initial fundraising, as they show investors the rigour of your analysis and the thoughtfulness with which you have approached planning your venture. Your financial projections provide you with an opportunity to demonstrate or present a case for why your venture is reasonably feasible from a business perspective. Developing a business model and subsequent estimations of future income and expenses will allow you to evaluate the basic validity of your business. Your financials are also a crucial fundraising tool. It is not uncommon that a VC or angel investor will ignore the numbers your financial projections produce early on, since they know that early projections rarely accurately predict a venture's future performance. What early investors *are* interested in, however, is whether your financial projections reflect sound and well-reasoned assumptions about how your business will operate.

As your venture begins to generate revenue, the financial statements and projection will become important tools for managing and measuring the progress of your venture. They will act as a report card for financial milestones, facilitating accountability, and the identification of potential financial risks. Understanding why your financial statements differ from your past financial projections will facilitate regular assessment of your fundamental assumptions and the ability to continually improve them.

So what do investors want to see? For the purpose of this section we will focus on the perspectives of two of the more common sources of startup financing: angel investors and venture capital firms. As such, the key characteristics you want to communicate in your financials are as follows:

- that you understand your market segment, market size, customer, and value of your product/service;
- that your product/service has the potential for massive growth;
- that you will invest an investor's money wisely;
- a four- to five-year forecast (first two years monthly, back three annually);
- that your company will show $50–100 million in revenue in Year 5 (this is not always necessary depending on the focus of the VC and your product/service).

Having these things covered doesn't mean investment is assured, but it *does* mean that you potentially have a competitive idea.

In the following sections we will go through the basics of your financial statements. It's crucial that any founder has a solid understanding of their finances and what they mean. Your financial statements consist of three fundamental components: the balance sheet, income statement, and cash flow statement. Each of these three components tells an investor something different about your company. Before we get into it, we'd like to provide you with a friendly public service announcement: investopedia.com is your friend. We consulted Investopedia often when going through the process of fundraising ourselves. Don't be afraid to look up what you don't know.

Financial statements: balance sheet

A company's balance sheet shows what the company owns, what it owes, and what is left over (assets, liabilities, equity). Assets are anything that can generate cash flow, reduce expenses, or improve sales – including machinery, patents, buildings, etc. Liabilities are what the company owes. Equity is any value left over after subtracting the liabilities from assets – essentially, the value of a company after covering what it owes.

So what does the balance sheet show you? The balance sheet is generally considered a snapshot of a company's general financial health at a specific point in time. It tells you the net worth of the business; what proportion of debts are due in the short term (less than one year) versus long term (greater than one year); and how values such as cash, accounts payable, accounts receivable, equity, inventory, or retained earnings change.

A balance sheet does not show you income or expenses over a period of time, but rather the current market value of any assets; the quality of any assets; contingent liabilities (potential liabilities if certain future conditions are not met); and operating lease obligations (the ability to purchase an asset at the end of the lease).

The basic format for a balance sheet is shown in Tables 12.1 and 12.2, broken down into 'Assets' and 'Liabilities and Equity'.

Table 12.1   Balance sheet assets

Assets	
Cash	A
Accounts receivable	B
Inventory	C
Prepaid expenses	D
Current assets	A+B+C+D = E
Other assets	F
Fixed assets at cost (PP&E)	G
Accumulated depreciation	H
Net fixed assets	G-H = I
Total assets	E+F+I = J

Table 12.2 Balance sheet liabilities and equity

Liabilities and equity	
Accounts payable	K
Accrued expenses	L
Current portion of debt	M
Income taxes payable	N
Current liabilities	K+L+M+N = O
Long-term debt	P
Capital stock	Q
Retained earnings	R
Shareholders' equity	Q+R = S
Total liabilities and equity	O+P+S = T

Financial statements: income statement

A company's income statement shows its sales, expenses and profitability over a period of time. It is generally updated monthly, quarterly and annually. So what does your income statement show you? It tells you if sales are going up or down; your gross profit; all expenses for the allotted time period; increases and decreases in net income; how much money is left to grow your business; how much money is left for the owner(s); and how much money is left to pay principal debts.

An income statement doesn't tell you whether your overall financial condition is strong or weak; the money owed to you (accounts receivable) or the money you owe (accounts payable); nor what you own (assets) or owe (liabilities). For this information, see the balance sheet.

The basic format for an income statement is shown in Table 12.3.

Financial statements: cash flow statement

A company's cash flow statement shows its sources, uses and balance of cash. It provides a report of all company activities

Table 12.3   Income statement

Income statement	
Net sales	A
Cost of goods sold	B
Gross profit	A-B = C
Sales and marketing	D
Research and development	E
General and administrative	F
Operating expenses	D+E+F = G
Income from operations	C-G = H
Interest income	I
Income taxes	J
Net income	H+I-J = K

that affect its cash over a period of time. These activities are broken into Operating, Investing and Financing. Fundamentally, it shows how your company uses its cash, and whether it has enough to keep running. Cash is crucial for ensuring the day-to-day viability of your company, from paying bills and salaries to routine expenses.

Think of it like this. You have an engine that generates solid fuel but runs on liquid fuel. That solid fuel is the value or revenue your company generates, and the cash is the liquid fuel your company needs to keep running. Your cash flow statement shows your liquid fuel consumption over time, and tells you if you need to convert more of that solid fuel into liquid fuel. Many companies may produce a profit, but don't have a positive cash flow.

So what does your cash flow statement show you? It displays whether your company has enough cash to cover day-to-day activities, pay debts on time, and maintain and grow the business without negative cash flow; whether your company needs additional working capital (cash) when sales increase; the maximum loan payment the business can afford; the breakdown of principal and interest on your loan payments; and potential weaknesses in your company's ability to keep cash and how you'll handle them.

Your cash flow statement will not provide how much you have in accounts receivable and accounts payable; your balance in assets, liabilities and net worth; or the depreciation of equipment or other assets. For this information, see the balance sheet.

The basic format for a cash flow statement is shown in Table 12.4.

Table 12.4 Cash flow statement

Cash flow statement	
Beginning cash balance	A
Cash receipts	B
Cash disbursements	C
Cash from operations	B-C = D
Fixed asset purchases	E
Net borrowings	F
Income taxes paid	G
Sale of stock	H
Ending cash balance	A+D-E+F-G+H = I

Figuring out who your investors should be

So, who is going to be investing in your company? At different stages in your venture, different stakeholders will be best positioned to invest. In general, early idea-stage funding might come through grants from schools and accelerators, family and friends, or angel investors. Later-stage funding generally comes from venture capital groups. Understanding who your potential investors are and what they're looking for is important for framing your business and collecting the kind of information that will position you best for raising funds. The following sections will provide some useful context for the types of investors at each stage and what they're looking for.

But before that, how does youth play into all of this? After all, that's what this book is all about; there are millions of 'How To' business books, but not one (at least not as far as we can tell) focuses on the specifics of youth entrepreneurship. Frankly, being young doesn't make fundraising any easier. As we've said a number of times, and will continue to say, investors care disproportionately about the composition of the founding team when making their investment decision. The most significant reason is, the younger you are, the less experience you're likely to have, and when it comes to startups and building a business there are few things that make up for a lack of experience. Now, that's not to say that youth can't run or build startups, but it means we, and you, have to be cognizant of our strengths and weaknesses, and account for that when building out our team. It's not for no reason that the average founder of the top 1 per cent of startups by growth is 45 years old. When broken down, founders under 29 account for just 10 per cent of the top 1 per cent of startups by growth, and 15 per cent of startups overall. According to a study out of MIT evaluating 2.7 million entrepreneurs, the average age of a founder who started a company that hired at least one employee is 41.9.[2]

Why do we bring this up? Surely it may not seem motivating, and indeed some of you may be reluctant to even pursue a startup after reading such figures (which is why we didn't start the book with this). There are two reasons: first, if you're going to be one of the successful startups, you need to be aware of your strengths and weaknesses, and build a team of founders, investors, advisors, and mentors that can compensate accordingly; second, youth entrepreneurship can look very different to how it's popularly conceptualized. Indeed, even if there was a complete certainty that your venture would fail, I would recommend that you proceed anyway. The experience you gain through trial and error will ensure that when you build something truly massive and world-changing, you already know largely what not to do. Having a small business operating off a Shopify account that you manage on weekends or after school is nothing less than fantastic, because it provides a basis for learning all the fundamentals of business that will be relevant to any future venture no matter how large. The point is to start something, and something of *value*. Our hope is that this book can provide you with some of the knowledge we and many other older and more successful entrepreneurs have learned through that process of trial and error so that you don't have to (as much).

Types of investors

Pre-seed stage

A company at the pre-seed stage is in the process of refining its business model, market-product fit and product. In the past, the only investors at this stage were the founders themselves, and perhaps family and friends. However, today there are other options like crowdfunding platforms (eg Kickstarter, Indiegogo) and government grants that are worth looking at. When it comes to investment, it's important that founders work to take the company as far as possible before looking outwards for investment. Oftentimes, the lack of funding at this stage forces examination of the product and its ability to sell itself (or the ability of the founders to sell it) without external support.

Seed stage

Seed funding is the first official funding stage a company will undergo. A company in seed stage is generally working on a proof of concept after launching or is in the process of launching a minimal viable product (MVP); often some manner of funding will be necessary for the development of the MVP and attracting early customers. This stage includes companies both pre- and post-revenue, though any revenue generated will likely be through paid pilot projects and very early adopters. At the seed stage, you'll find a number of different investors, including governments, accelerators, academic institutions, family and friends, crowdfunding platforms, angel investors, and even some VC firms. Seed funding generally varies from $500,000 to $5 million depending on the company, with roughly two-thirds of seed rounds between $1 and $5 million and company valuations anywhere from $3 to $8 million.[3]

Growth stage

Growth-stage funding includes Series A, B, C and beyond. These are generally for companies that show early traction, a solid business model, and significant growth potential. Series A funding investors look for companies prepared for venture capital.

A *Series A* funding round generally occurs once a business has developed a base of early adopters and is looking to rapidly scale and further refine their product or service. On average, Series A funding ranges from $5 to $25 million.

Series B funding is for businesses looking to scale rapidly. At this point companies have a refined product and are looking to enter new markets quickly. The average Series B funding round is just under $22.5 million, and on occasion Series B funding rounds reach upwards of $70 million.

Series C funding is generally reserved for successful companies looking to develop new products, acquire other companies, or expand into global markets. Series C funding rounds are considered late stage, and are often led by hedge funds, investment banks, private equity firms, and other major institutional investors.

Smart money

Now more than ever, fundraising is about far more than just money. No, we don't mean the value signalling that comes with announcing the size of your latest funding round, or evaluating the quality of a company, its team, or an idea based on how much they secured in fundraising. Rather, it's the soft value that an investor can provide that makes all the difference. Choosing an investor that has a better network, more expertise, but offers less funding is almost always the best bet. As VC, seed and pre-seed stage funding has become more competitive, investors have begun to realize that if they're going to compete successfully for investment, they need to do more than simply offer a cheque. They need to offer expertise, a network and advisorship; they have to offer real value that helps you grow your company. It makes intuitive sense, because the more value an early-stage investor can offer you, the more likely you are to succeed, and everyone benefits. Yet, in a world of value signalling and competition to raise more than the next person, turning down a larger pay cheque for a more experienced and uniquely beneficial investor is difficult to do. This is particularly important for youth, who more often than not don't have the benefit of significant experience and expertise of their own to rely on.

Notes

1 Spence, R (2013) Entrepreneurs aren't the only business leaders who don't understand finance, *Financial Post*, https://financialpost.com/entrepreneur/entrepreneurs-arent-the-only-business-leaders-who-dont-understand-finance (archived at https://perma.cc/85YD-PWZE)

2 Azoulay, P et al (2018) Age and high-growth entrepreneurship, *American Economic Review*, 2 (1), pp 65–82

3 Glasner, J (2021) North American startup funding was on fire in Q1, *Crunchbase News*, https://news.crunchbase.com/news/na-startup-funding-on-fire-in-q1/ (archived at https://perma.cc/N6PU-CW5A)

13
Scaling and exit strategy

If you have ever visited a startup blog, read startup Q&As on Quora, or just spent enough time entering your startup questions into Google, you will have most definitely come across the term 'scaling' no less than 1,000 times. So what *is* scaling, why can't we just call it growing, and why are we supposed to care so much about it?

In your search for information, you may have also come across a remote corner, home to a resource called *Y Combinator*. Y Combinator (YC) is legendary in the startup world for helping Airbnb, Dropbox, Twitch, Weebly, Quora, Reddit, and countless other massively successful companies get started. Their advice actually when it comes to building a startup is 'do things that don't scale'. This means that in order for your venture to gain momentum, you must first do (or consider doing) laborious and rather unglamorous tasks like recruiting users and addressing narrow markets. For those of you that have not read the blogs of YC's founder, Paul Graham, he offers sage advice on numerous startup-related topics and serves as a valuable source of information for founders.[1]

So, you have a religion of scaling on one hand and advice to start by doing things that don't scale on the other. Do not fret about this very reasonable and understandable confusion. Things will make sense shortly.

What is scaling?

Scaling is taking a market-validated product or service and growing the customer base and revenue at a rapid pace to reach profitability as quickly as possible. So in essence, scaling does mean growing, but as is true in all other things startup-related, it needed its own term. That said, scaling in start-up speak is about growth at an incredibly rapid pace. This is a key difference between startups and other businesses because startups are fundamentally engineered to scale and do so quickly, while other businesses grow at a more conservative, sustainable speed. The key to scaling is to keep operating costs relatively stable while escalating revenues as much as possible. Naturally, this is challenging to do and scaling is an exceptionally trying period for an entrepreneur during which your company will be stress-tested across every possible dimension.

Preparing to scale

The key to preparing your venture for this period of growth is, as Paul Graham at Y Combinator put, to do things that don't scale. The idea is that many of the things you need to do to ensure that your company is well positioned to undergo extreme growth aren't in and of themselves scalable. An easy example of this would be to recruit users manually, by literally going out, talking to people, and trying to get them to interact with your product or service. This is clearly not something that a founder or anyone in a quickly growing business will feel they have the time to undertake, but early on this crucial step can bring a company to a point of critical mass where referrals and less labour-intensive forms of customer acquisition drive increasingly rapid growth.

What are the other things you as a founder can do to ensure your venture is optimally positioned for scaling?

- Consider doing things manually until you can write the code, build the partnerships or outsource the manufacturing to automate it.

- Focus on providing each and every early adopter with as much attention as you can possibly muster; focus on a small initial market with a dedicated narrow user base.

These strategies, and strategies similar to them, fine-tune your approach as quickly as possible, and develop a core user base of die-hard customers. These seemingly tedious and unscalable strategies exist to facilitate one thing – you are able to learn about your customers' wants and needs enough to build a product that they and others cannot say no to.

Team and culture

The next crucial preparation before scaling is to ensure you have the best possible team to do so. A well-coordinated and highly functioning team is crucial to withstanding the tremendous stress and pressure of growing rapidly. Having clear responsibilities established for each individual is key, and it is often worth spending extra time to ensure your first few employees are of the highest quality.

Third, and perhaps a piece of advice you will hear less often – focus on culture. In the trying times of extreme growth, ensuring that early employees are not only behind the mission of your company, but feel as if they are embedded within a cohesive culture, is essential. Analysts suggest that in the next several years, culture will become more important to potential hires than salary. Indeed, this is often the allure of startups when compared with corporate behemoths; they are small enough that you can really focus on building not only a company, but an environment and culture that people love. This will keep people engaged in your startup through the trying times, acting like glue when everything else might be falling apart. People have to feel that they are a *part* of something, that they are valued, that they have a voice, and that they have power; the process of scaling is the easiest time to lose sight of that. The idea that the fiduciary duty of company executives to shareholders supersedes any duty to employees, or more broadly to society is, in our opinion and experience, fundamentally wrong. Worse than that, we believe that this notion is actually incredibly harmful. Such an ethos creates a culture in which productivity is the goal above all else; a mindset and culture that leaves little space for focusing on the well-being and needs of employees. If you want to learn more about fostering collaboration, make sure to check out Chapter 9.

A Harvard Business School study illustrates the importance of an almost obsessive focus on culture fit and employee character.[2] In an evaluation of more than 50,000 workers, two things were determined: first, toxic workers are *much* more productive than the average worker (note that this does not mean that all productive workers are toxic); and second, avoiding toxic workers altogether (aka not hiring them), even those that are 'superstars' (in the top 1 per cent of productivity), is *always* in the best interest of your company.

A toxic worker is an individual who engages in behaviour that is harmful to an organization, including either its property or people. Through the effects of their downstream toxic behaviour – such as creating lower productivity among other workers, creating a culture of rule breaking, increasing employee turnover – toxic workers, no matter how productive they are on average, cost companies thousands of dollars over the long term. If companies opt to focus on productivity over employee character or culture fit, this problem only exacerbates. Hiring toxic workers because productivity is prioritized means that employee turnover increases, which in a tight job market means the pressure to hire the first person to come through the door increases. Thus, a positive feedback loop develops that undermines culture, increases the toxicity of the workplace, decreases productivity, and cripples your company.

In the process of scaling, speed and efficiency become a sort of religion, and focusing on worker culture or employee character become seemingly trivial in the face of a 'deliver or die' environment. Particularly in competitive job markets as well, being picky about who to employ past ensuring they have the necessary skills is often considered a luxury – but this and other studies illustrate that it is crucial for long-term success, and that the *quality of an individual should not be ignored*.

Now we entirely understand that culture and character are difficult to characterize, and even more difficult to identify or measure. And that many of the strategic practices necessary to scaling effectively are those that involve 'soft' topics that often seem nebulous or 'fluffy'. Many entrepreneurs are technical – they have an affinity for the sort of brute problem solving so often required of engineers or computer scientists. To ask such people to focus instead on prioritizing something as vague or incalculable as 'culture' seems silly. The culture of entrepreneurship typically praises STEM disciplines above all else; we are told throughout school that the ability to calculate and quantify, to measure and optimize, is fundamental to getting a job or remaining competitive in school.

The origin stories we hear about successful founders involve hacking software together in dorm rooms and building motherboards in garages. And yet, we are fundamentally social beings! While all those things are certainly beneficial and important, building a successful and resilient company requires something more – the ability to lead people, people who need a sense of purpose, a sense of community, and a strong sense of culture in order to do their jobs efficiently and effectively. Humans want certainty, and the ability to easily quantify things makes them tangible and less uncertain. It is easier to focus on maximizing productivity than it is culture. Quinn has had the fortune of speaking with Dr Jeffrey Pfeffer from the Stanford Graduate School of Business, who, on the topic of workplace well-being and employee culture, has spoken often about how companies don't do anything about these issues (even though they know they should) because they don't know where to start. These problems seem too large, too daunting, and too difficult to understand or quantify. But more than ever before, evidence shows us just how important it is that we try to tackle them all the same. It is exactly the problem that Autumn was starting to solve; by making the psychological well-being of individuals in companies measurable, we make it manageable, reorienting companies around optimizing for the well-being of their employees (and consequently, the long-term success of their company).

Exit strategy

An exit strategy is the transferral of a portion, or whole ownership, of a company from one party to another. Investors, or any other equity holders, only see the returns on their investments or the value of their shares once their ownership stake is acquired by another party.

There are many different types of exit strategies, so we will go through the major tactics with an explanation of the general benefits and downsides of each. It is important that you as a founder have an exit strategy in mind from the very beginning of your business. Positioning yourself and your company strategically for one type of exit or another can greatly increase the ultimate value of your company and ensure that you are compensated well for the value you have created.

Initial public offering

The first type of exit is the initial public offering (IPO). An IPO is when a privately owned company offers a portion of its shares to the public marketplace. This is often done as a strategy for growing companies to raise funds quickly, or for larger companies to facilitate the exit of investors or other major shareholders. The advantages of an IPO are that the company can quickly raise funds down the road through a 'secondary offering' or the release of more privately held shares to the public marketplace; compensation can be provided to employees through stock that is more easily sold than stock in a privately held company, which consequently is a better method for attracting talent; mergers and acquisitions may become easier because of the simplicity with which public stock can be purchased and valuations can be assessed; and finally, an IPO conveys prestige and credibility, which may improve business in general. Public offerings are not without their downsides, however, as they are accompanied by significantly more governance oversight; they can distract management from focusing on improving real financial results; they are incredibly expensive to execute; and they can force the disclosure of important business practices that may aid competition through regular and publicly available filings to the Securities and Exchange Commission (SEC).

Merger or acquisition

The second category of exits is mergers and acquisitions. A merger involves the combining of two separate, similarly sized entities into a new joint organization. Mergers are very uncommon, since rarely do two companies stand to benefit from giving up some measure of autonomy to merge with one another. An acquisition is the purchase of one entity by another entity. There are many different categories of mergers and acquisitions, which greatly affect the ultimate organization of the new joint company or acquired one. For this reason we will not go much further into the benefits or disadvantages of each, other than to say mergers and acquisitions can vary from incredibly beneficial to downright disastrous. A common form of exit for smaller startups, particularly in the technology space, is through acquisition or an acqui-hire. An acqui-hire is an acquisition in which the founders and team members of the acquired company become employees of the larger company, oftentimes with the role of integrating their technology or talent into the parent company.

Private offering

The third exit strategy is the private offering. A private offering is the sale of a company to private individuals or organizations in an effort to raise funds. In this scenario, existing shareholders can be partially or entirely bought out in the new fundraising round. Private offerings are difficult for any larger company because fewer investors have the sort of capital necessary to purchase a larger company. Generally, a private offering can be considered to have the same advantages and disadvantages as fundraising, which were discussed in the previous chapter.

Buy back

The last exit strategy we will cover in this chapter is when the company buys out an investor directly. This can either happen if the company is a 'cash cow' or through the use of debt instruments. 'Cash cow' essentially refers to a company that generates such substantial sums of liquid assets (cash) that it can afford to purchase shares from the equity holder itself. When a company buys out an investor without the ability to do so through cash generated, it can be completed through the use of debt, whereby a company acquires a loan to buy out an investor, taking on a liability in the process.

The last and most frequent question when it comes to an exit strategy is 'When is the right time to exit?' There are two general responses to this question. The short answer is that there is no definitively right time. The long answer is that it entirely depends on what the founders and investors are looking for – an exit might be forced on a company by an investor looking to get a return, or it might be a founder looking to move on to something new. In each scenario, there are different things to consider and different interests to account for. This is in part why having an exit strategy from the very beginning is important; it will inform many future decisions for you as a founder, from the sort of investors you bring on, to the sort of founders and employees you hire – you have to know what you want, and you have to have a vision and plan for how to get there.

Notes

1 Graham, P (2013) Do Things that Don't Scale, *paulgraham.com,* http://paulgraham.com/ds.html (archived at https://perma.cc/ YYF4-DV4R)

2 Housman, M and Minor, D (2015) Toxic Workers, Harvard Business School Working Paper 16-057, https://doi. org/10.2139/ssrn.2677700 (archived at https://perma.cc/5X5U-DHCD)

Part Three
Ecosystem

14
The Entrepreneurial Community

An ecosystem in ecology is defined as a biological community of interacting organisms and their physical environment. In many ways, an entrepreneurial ecosystem functions similarly. The term has become mainstream in business since it was first coined by James Moore in a 1993 issue of the *Harvard Business Review*. As he described it originally, companies should not be categorized as constituents of one specific industry, but rather as part of a *business ecosystem* that spans a multitude of different industries.[1]

In a business ecosystem, 'companies coevolve capabilities around a new innovation: they work cooperatively and competitively to support new products, satisfy customer needs, and eventually incorporate the next round of innovations'.[2] A more modern definition of an entrepreneurial ecosystem is a general community of founders exchanging knowledge and experience amongst each other, each person feeding off one another for inspiration to continue along in the journey of building a business. As Parmvir Singh of yecommunity.com explains it, the best ecosystems are mechanisms that internally transfer '... concepts, talent and resources. The overall result is that moments of brilliance and invention are more consistent, through networking and knowledge sharing'.[3] Ecosystems typically consist of all stakeholders involved in the operation of a business, from suppliers and distributors to competitors. The next two chapters will focus particularly on entrepreneurial ecosystems. To learn more about them, we will be taking a look at these guiding questions:

1 What is the importance of having an ecosystem?

2 Where does the ecosystem of legitimate and real entrepreneurs exist?

3 How can you engage with them?

4 How can you build a personal brand that feeds back into your business?

5 How can you give back to the larger ecosystem?

6 How is the ecosystem going to change in the future?

What is the importance of having an ecosystem?

The value of having an ecosystem as a founder cannot be understated. In Chapter 2, we discussed in great depth how entrepreneurship is fundamentally a lonely process. As founders, we must come to terms with this fact and find ways to manage working alone for a great deal of time. That being said, we can find solace in knowing that we're not alone in this experience. There are countless fellow entrepreneurs within your city, your province (or state) and country who are dealing with the same self-doubt, family pressures, and other anxieties that you battle concurrently while developing your business. Plugging into an ecosystem of entrepreneurs will remind you of this companionship even when you may not directly feel it during your work. Another benefit of engaging in an entrepreneurial ecosystem is that you can establish helpful and sensible partnership(s) that will later prove beneficial to sales. Your company will receive much-needed support in terms of recognition when other companies with complementary areas of expertise are able to refer you to their respective customer base. For instance, Surf was able to set up partnerships with companies such as the LVE Group, Hawke Media and Juice Labs to name a few. These three organizations would help their customers by telling them how Surf could be used to address some of their specific audience management issues, and in turn, Surf would spread the word about these organizations to its customers. It's worth mentioning that if these companies were in vastly different industries with customers that come to them with contrasting needs, it would not be practical for a partnership of this nature to exist. You would not expect a partnership between Western Union and Subway, because each company offers something that's in no way related to the other (financial services compared to a restaurant), which makes this a nonviable partnership.

Connecting with an ecosystem of entrepreneurs can also aid in fundraising efforts and building up your advisory board. Simply put, a company will find it much more difficult to assemble the best talent, stay relevant for innovation purposes, and secure an adequate level of funding if it's not associated with some type of ecosystem within its geographic area. Imagine if you owned the only startup in your town. Would there be a great deal of interest among investors, or would they have enough of an incentive to contribute capital to your business? You would most likely appear as a risky investment in an unestablished area that contains little to no consumer demand; after all, why else would there be an absence of competition operating in your locality?

An identifiable ecosystem can provide a business with credibility, a universal requirement by investors and advisors before they even consider dedicating their time and resources to your company. These investors and advisors can be found within the ecosystem already, either as current shareholders or former executives of a company in the community. When there is an active ecosystem that exists in a certain place, people will eventually take notice and gravitate towards it in hopes of getting in on the action in any way they can. Such was the case in 2018, when Amazon announced its shortlist of 20 cities it was considering for the site of its second headquarters. Cities did everything possible to attract the company – which vowed to introduce 50,000 jobs and spend $5 billion in the city that it chose – including some mayors writing 1,000 Amazon product reviews, and other mayors offering to change town names to 'Amazon'.[4] In an interview with the *Washingtonian*, Holly Sullivan, the Amazon executive who led the search for the company's next headquarters, justified the decision to choose Crystal City, Virginia (the winner of the Amazon sweepstakes), saying, 'We needed to find a location that has the resources and the sort of education ecosystem to build upon that tech-talent pipeline'.[5] Evidently, associating your company with a distinguishable ecosystem is a worthy pursuit, as it can reap rewards in the form of attracting coveted investors and advisors who want to become involved with a potential gold mine.

Where does the ecosystem of legitimate and real entrepreneurs exist?

Perhaps you have now reached the point of wondering where you can locate and access this community of like-minded individuals. Do your research about places and events where entrepreneurs congregate. This includes anything from keynote presentations to panel discussions held by founders on a topic that will be applicable to the majority of entrepreneurs. Use platforms like LinkedIn, Facebook Events pages, and simple web searches to your advantage. For LinkedIn, reach out to your current network and also people you don't know yet who are entrepreneurs and ask them about entrepreneurship-related events. If you see a LinkedIn post about a particular activity on your feed, ask the author about the event, their experience, and other similar events they're planning on attending. Don't be afraid to ask people on social networking sites for help in this way; they have no reason not to convey this information to you and may be impressed by your ambition. Of your research results, find the time to attend some of the events in your city. If you truly want to become a part of the ecosystem, it's important that you show your face because other entrepreneurs will take notice of your dedication. That said, you should not attend every single event that you come across because your time is a scarce resource that can be used for other purposes. You don't want to be the founder known for not valuing your time as much as you should. Take a cost-benefit approach for each occasion, placing your priority on those meetings that will bring out the people who are most involved in your area's entrepreneurial ecosystem. These individuals will have the capability to connect you with people who have the network and wisdom possibly to accelerate your company's growth.

In this search for a community of real entrepreneurs there will be a pivotal moment that requires you to exercise good judgment and decision-making ability: not all entrepreneurs are legitimate. Many will claim that they're in the business of providing a certain service or some innovative product, using their website or social media to project exaggerated figures in sales or number of people impacted. Although you may want to immerse yourself in an ecosystem of accomplished entrepreneurs, don't be easily swayed by a company presenting itself as doing exceedingly well. Employ caution before engaging with an entrepreneur who is overly confident or boastful about the success and trajectory of their business, as this is one of the most apparent signs of an illegitimate entrepreneur. They speak about their company in a way that is visibly emotionally charged, which makes them unable to take criticism about it. You may have noticed this in individuals you have dealt with in the past, who brush off the advice they receive for their work by saying, 'I knew that already' and demonstrate stubbornness in the decisions they make for a collective group. Conversely, authentic entrepreneurs carry themselves in a humble manner and exude an appropriate level of confidence when talking about their company. They do this in a way that makes the listener feel that the founder is secure about their business and its performance. They're honest about their company's hardships, and they're self-aware when it comes to possible areas of improvement which their business has yet to achieve. These founders have this sense of security because they're able to detach their personal identity from the business that they're building (as discussed in Chapter 6), which brings them a level of mental peace that is vital to pursuing entrepreneurship as a full-time career.

Perhaps you're still unsure about whether or not an entrepreneur you're interested in speaking to is legitimate. In this scenario, you can directly message the individual (try using a social media platform) and ask to get on a five- to ten-minute call with them. If they accept, you will be able to gauge the person's behaviour when they discuss their business and respond to any of the questions you have. During the conversation, be sure to take what they say in terms of their company's performance with a grain of salt, especially if there's no way to fact check their metrics and estimates. Be gracious for their time (after all, they didn't owe you anything) and following this brief interaction, you can then decide if you would like to create and maintain a relationship with this person. Perhaps you're *still* unsure about the validity of this entrepreneur, and you're considering meeting them. Before you commit to an in-person interaction, it's worthwhile asking for a second opinion about their reputation amongst other entrepreneurs in your ecosystem. If multiple sources convey warnings, citing negative experiences with them in the past, then you should distance yourself from this individual. Keep in mind that your reputation is the central piece of information that people know (or discover) about you. Your reputation is a direct by-product of the way you make people feel as well as the individuals you surround yourself with. Don't tarnish your reputation by associating yourself with others who have considerably poor reputations.

How can you engage with the community?

Once you have established those entrepreneurs with whom you would like to connect and cultivate relationships, think about how you're going to do this. Specifically, how can you engage with people? Our advice is this: when you meet somebody, in person or online, it's *very important to listen*. As much as you might be tempted to try and communicate everything that is inside your head... that won't help you! You won't learn anything, and you certainly won't leave a good impression on the other person. People can immediately tell whether you're speaking to them out of an interest in their story, or just wanting to pitch or sell something to them – and nobody likes to be trapped in an unsolicited sales pitch.

What you really want to do is *listen* to their story, their interests, why they came to the event or online space – and try to find commonalities. Where do your interests and goals overlap? How might you be able to help them? What might be the foundation of a relationship with them? Then you can go from there.

Tips for in-person meetings

When going to events, the importance of following up with the people you meet cannot be stressed enough. How many times have you attended an event, exchanged tons of business cards, gone home and done absolutely nothing with them? The chances of someone just looking into their pocket and reaching out to someone who hands them a business card is quite low. Instead, jot down their information and then a week from that event you follow up with something along the lines of, 'Hey, I don't know if you remember me, but we had a conversation about X, I would love to meet for coffee for 10 to 15 minutes and follow up the conversation from there.'

There lies the simplicity when reaching out to an individual for a second interaction, but you would be surprised as to how many people do this incorrectly. Once you have sent this message, you have to be comfortable with the possible reality that the individual may not respond. While it can be appropriate to follow up a few days later with a similar message, you must realize when to step away and prevent yourself from appearing desperate or creating unwanted feelings of pressure for the person. Chances are if the individual hasn't responded to your second message, they will almost certainly not reply the third time around.

Tips for virtual meetings

Whenever you're engaging with someone through an online platform, keep it concise. Tell the person a bit about your own story (think two to three sentences regarding who you are, and what you're doing), but make sure as much as possible that you get *right to the point*. Why *exactly* are you reaching out? What do you want from this person and when do you want it (designate a clear date and time)? A lot of people don't have time on their hands; they're going to look at your message quickly, and if they're not able to figure out exactly what you're asking for and whether they can respond speedily... they just won't. You need to make it easy for people to get back to you. Be as straightforward as possible when it comes to your overarching ask, so that people can respond with a simple yes or no, rather than an open-ended inquiry for which they will have to dedicate more time than they would like.

Especially for entrepreneurs that you're adamant about reaching, you must establish multiple touchpoints with them. This means that you're not only sending emails, but you're also sending regular LinkedIn messages, Instagram messages, directly tagged tweets, and however else the entrepreneur communicates with their audience. Rather than just directly messaging the person, try engaging with the content that they publish online by commenting on their most recent posts. This doesn't mean that you comment with a forgettable emoji that the individual will simply scroll past, but instead that you comment with something of value, which relates to the content itself. People who publish original content to public platforms have undoubtedly devoted time to their work, and when you exhibit your genuine interest in whatever they shared, you're acknowledging their time and effort, which is something that most people will remember about you. In addition, by engaging with their content online in this manner, you're generating traffic to their posts which serves as a benefit to them. Another useful tactic that can help the outreach process is asking a mutual contact to create a group chat consisting of the three of you (the individual of interest, the contact, and yourself) in which your contact can introduce you. An example of successful execution in outreach is when Swish attempted to contact one of his heroes in entrepreneurship, Gary Vaynerchuck, every day for six months via email and Twitter, with various comments and critiques about Gary's YouTube show *DailyVee*. Swish also created another touchpoint with Gary by directly contacting his assistant David Rock, which may have been extremely effective as he is constantly in Gary's ear. Note that even though he was reaching out with value-added comments on a daily basis, Swish did so with no expectation of receiving anything in return, which meant that he was not disappointed whenever Gary didn't respond. As one of Gary's famous quotes states, '*Giving* means giving without the expectation of return'. For his dedication, Swish was eventually able to schedule a meeting with Gary in New York. The lesson from Swish's experience is not to be repetitive in your messages to the person you're looking to gain the attention of, but rather to provide consistent doses of value in every type of communication you send.

Notes

1 Moore, JF (1993) Predators and prey: A new ecology of competition, *Harvard Business Review*, https://hbr.org/1993/05/predators-and-prey-a-new-ecology-of-competition (archived at https://perma.cc/VR53-VRN3)

2 Ibid

3 Singh, P (2018) Why is it important to build a startup ecosystem? *Ye!* https://social.yecommunity.com/news/390350 (archived at https://perma.cc/997Q-G4K6)

4 Liao, S (2017) The eight most outrageous things cities did to lure Amazon for HQ2, *The Verge*, https://www.theverge.com/2017/10/19/16504042/amazon-hq2-second-headquarters-most-funny-crazy-pitches-proposals-stonecrest-new-york (archived at https://perma.cc/FZ57-ADKD)

5 Mullins, L and Peischel, W (2019) Virginia drew an actual map for Amazon to influence Washington, *Washingtonian*, https://www.washingtonian.com/2019/05/30/virginia-drew-an-actual-map-for-amazon-to-influence-washington/ (archived at https://perma.cc/85EB-9P8V)

15
Marketing yourself effectively

Personal branding can be a great way to drive revenue into your company and build a network. A strong personal brand can mean that more people are interested in your ideas and business – for example, reputable figures like Gary Vaynerchuk have done an amazing job of creating a personal brand online. Because he captures people's attention, this has translated to more people visiting Gary's digital agencies for advice and business consulting, buying his books, and attending the events he speaks at.

The value of establishing your personal brand for the purpose of generating business leads is further explained by Ron Tite, founder and CEO of marketing agency Church+State, and host of a podcast called *The Coup*. We interviewed him for insight on how he built his personal brand and how it has helped his businesses. He tells us:

> To truly build a strong personal brand, you need to be continuously learning and leading in your field of expertise. Social media is critical because it allows you to efficiently

consume media that inspires and informs you. It empowers you to scale the helpful advice and content from those who share your thinking. It enables you to distribute your own original thinking and creativity, and it allows you to connect, communicate with, be challenged by, and champion those in your community who are on your side. When all of that is combined, you will grow and scale your personal brand.

Now that we know how beneficial social media can be for establishing your personal brand, the underlying question still remains: how can *you* build a personal brand that feeds back into your business? While there are books about this, here are some practical ways to get started:

- **Pick a platform** (eg LinkedIn, Instagram, Twitter, Medium, or any other relevant social media vehicle that caters to your preferences). Ideally, you should use a platform that plays to your strengths – so if you're a writer, go to Medium and LinkedIn; if you're someone who excels in photo and video, go to Facebook or Instagram. Don't spend time wondering which platform you should be on. Instead, ask yourself which platform are you most likely to derive more of a following or influence on, as this is the platform that will be most valuable to you. It's futile to spend a great deal of time choosing a platform because this decision can always be altered later based on what you feel is working for you. Instead, more emphasis should be placed on the next action listed here.

- **Start creating content.** As much as possible, good advice is to get into a routine for posting content. Think about what kind of content you want to post: Is it inspirational content that aims to get people to think outside of what they're currently doing? Do you want to be informative, or to give people a deeper insight into the industry you're focusing on? Similar to the first action, post content that plays to your strengths – if you're great at writing, publish an article or blog post. If you're a great storyteller and love speaking in front of others, film a video of yourself speaking about a relevant topic alone in your room, or in front of an audience in the form of a keynote presentation. Are you a great storyteller but hate the spotlight? Turn the camera off and record an audio podcast discussing any topic, or interview a particular guest. There are so many forms of content with different variations on each. The decision about which form of content to produce ultimately boils down to which type you're most comfortable creating because your audience will tune into any form of content as long as it's giving them quality information about something they're interested in.

- **Make it personal.** As much as possible, our advice is to ensure that people who are consuming your posts know that you're also a human, one who has similar aspirations and has faced similar situations to themselves.

- **Think about the 5 Cs.** The five Cs of *social media growth* are: content, community, consistency, context, and collaboration.

Bonus tip

Don't be afraid of mixing up your content format by posting various versions of the same piece of information to the applicable platform (eg posting a video on Instagram and transcribing the audio into an article for LinkedIn). This cross-platform strategy will enable you to reach as many people as possible with your content.

The 5 Cs of social media growth

Content

The quality of your personal brand is highly dependent on the content that you present to your audience, which encompasses not only the information within the content, but also the way you convey it to them. In order for your audience to recognize your personal brand, they need to *feel a connection* to you. This happens when the viewer believes that you're a source they can trust. According to Ron, he builds this trust by being:

> ... completely transparent with my audience about three things: 1) I want to responsibly draw the line between blatant self-promotion and simply informing those who like my perspective where they can get more, 2) I disclose anything that might be a bias, 3) I don't always get it right. A pitch slap to one person is a suggestion to another so none of us can please all the people all the time. Still, as a guiding principle, I try to earn the right to celebrate our accomplishments by adding far more value than I extract. It's pretty simple, really. Count your posts. How many talk about you or your company and how many add value or celebrate others without even subtle hints of what you do? If it's not 90 per cent of the latter, you're doing it wrong.

Additionally, your audience will feel a connection to you if they deem your content to be valuable. Valuable content typically falls into three buckets: *informative, inspirational*, and *personal anecdotes*. Which will you post? Which will you interact with? Will it be a mix, or will you specialize?

Informative content

Every single person in this world knows something, whether it be about the field they're studying or working in, or simply a topic they're deeply interested in. What's something that you can effortlessly talk about for hours on end? Whatever that topic is, you can be an informative source who shares your knowledge with other people. Perhaps you feel apprehensive doing this because you fear the potential judgement of others around you. Although this is a mindset that you must break out of, there are alternatives to get around this obstacle. Instead, consider sharing the thoughts of other people in the space, by reposting their content on LinkedIn or retweeting it on Twitter. There is no restriction in quoting someone, or profiling somebody else and sharing their story with the world (granted this information can be verified). Something that Swish did initially was pose discussion questions on LinkedIn. One of the first questions he put out on the platform was 'what is Bitcoin?' Soon after, several people began commenting under his post, which became a sort of public forum of information related to this topic. The reality is that people love talking about what they know because they take pride in this knowledge or enjoy teaching other people about something. Sharing other creators' content and asking discussion questions are great ways to initially side-step the task of producing your own content. That said, the worst thing to do when sharing another person's profile is to not add any original commentary to it on your behalf. There are news networks like CNN and Bloomberg for this purpose. Your job is not to relay another person's content but rather to add your own take to the story. Your audience wants to know why you're sharing the story, what lessons they can take away from it, and what lessons you derived from it (particularly the personal experiences you have tied to the story).

Inspirational content

When you think of inspirational content you might associate an image of a motivational speaker, telling you to follow your dreams. Instead, inspirational content can be found in the amazing stories of the people around you. Every person knows someone who has an incredibly unique story of perseverance and determination. Rather than confining these stories to your immediate friends and family, why not share such empowering stories to your network? When we alter our mindset about social media platforms as social networking sites, we are no longer afraid of putting content out and trying new things. The purpose of these social networking platforms should be to connect with people, not by sending them a connection or follow request, but rather by providing them with upfront value before they ask for it. By creating content that acts as vessels of exposure for people you admire or would like to network with, perhaps by profiling them through an interview, you're giving them a greater incentive to form a relationship with you. It bears repeating: people love talking about themselves and what they know, and this form of content is a far more effective way to connect with someone than the generic meeting for coffee.

Personal anecdotes

The most difficult piece of content to execute is personal anecdotes, or stories that you have about your past experiences. It goes a long way for the viewer when your content is intimate and personal to you. You want the people who are viewing your content to know that you're also a human who has similar aspirations, who has been in situations similar to those that they have experienced. To the extent that you're comfortable, don't hesitate to be vulnerable with your audience by expressing your mistakes or failures because they will feel a stronger inclination towards you for this authenticity. There are people out there who will applaud you for your courage, and will engage with your content more often simply because you're willing to be more transparent with them. We know it can be difficult to talk about your past failures, hardships, or moments of distress. What you must understand is that these experiences, of stress, poor time management, and even depression (poor mental health), may be very relatable to the viewer. You may feel like these issues are singular, that you're the only person who has gone through these situations, and consequently you feel discomfort in sharing them. It's oddly uplifting just how many people struggle with issues similar to you; all it takes is for you to put your authentic self out there, and see what happens. Again, sharing these stories and experiences is based on your comfort level, so don't feel pressured to reveal this information for the purpose of developing your personal brand.

Community

Especially in your early stages of building a personal brand, establishing a respectful and loyal community requires you to *engage with your community* every chance you get. This means not only posting, but also replying to comments on your posts, commenting on other people's posts, and actively joining the conversation. Replying to people that leave comments on your posts, that share their ideas and opinions about your content, is paramount. To these people, who might undervalue the significance of their comments in developing your community, it goes a long way when you interact with and acknowledge every comment you receive. It tells them there's another human behind the post that they're having a conversation on, and it will make them more likely to leave another comment the next time that you post. Developing a community starts with, but doesn't end with, only your posts. You should make it a routine to comment on as many other posts as possible, particularly the content that's relevant to your area of expertise. For instance, if you're running a daily motivation and inspiration Instagram page, the size of your community would expand immensely if you were to comment on the most recent posts of the five to ten leading Instagram pages within your motivation genre. As previously mentioned, thoughtful commenting does not involve simply throwing a couple of emojis at them... aim for well-crafted comments that actually show that you took the time to read through the publisher's material. You could even consider taking the conversation offline – think about getting on five-minute calls with five people that commented on your latest post. With enough consistency, you will garner curiosity from the audience of the top pages within your category, who are already interested in the subject matter of your content, and therefore will likely follow you once they discover your page. These large pages in your genre may even decide to repost one of your pieces of content on their story if prompted by the amount of continued support you show to their posts. If you're hoping for this kind of referral, you need to understand that you cannot realistically expect other content creators to care about you or your personal brand without you first acknowledging their efforts (even then, it's not guaranteed that they will support you in return).

Make a point as well of targeting specific groups or communities of people who will relate to your backstory, and will relate to your message. Every single individual has a unique story, just as they have certain topics that they're interested in. Whatever your backstory is, perhaps growing up without a father, or as an immigrant, there are other people out there with similar stories who will see themselves in you and your experiences. Sharing your posts with these groups will strengthen your online community, and you will provide them with much-needed representation. The best aspect of community is that you typically get back what you invest into it, which means that remaining consistent in posting your content, actively engaging with your audience on your posts, and showing a clear interest in the content of others can go a long way towards growing your community in an organic manner. Ultimately, community is going to be the greatest be all and end all for whether you're going to be successful in telling your story, sharing your brand, and spreading your message to people. Building a community has helped founders like Ron tremendously as it directly contributes to cultivating a personal brand. Ron describes these benefits, stating:

> I have a number of businesses and my personal brand has directly or indirectly grown revenue in all of them. Some are pretty easy to quantify. My growing speaking revenue plus my book and TV deals are all directly related to my personal brand. But I'd argue that my exposure activities are responsible for the leads which created revenue for Church+State. Obviously, that revenue isn't created if the team doesn't execute but they don't get to execute if the phone doesn't ring.

Consistency

Imagine if an influencer that you follow on social media was to maintain a regular weekly posting schedule for a month, before seemingly disappearing for four months, without any communication during that time. Naturally, you and many other members of their audience would forget about them and occupy your time with some other form of content. Unless you're one of the most prominent figures in the space, losing the interest of your audience, even momentarily, can have detrimental results for your personal brand. People don't want to follow people who only surface on the internet every four months, especially if you're making promises about posting that you cannot keep. They want to follow people that are ideally posting two to three times per week, if not every day. That doesn't mean you need to force yourself to post, because this will produce a lack of authenticity that will be reflected in the audience's viewing experience. Only post when you have something to say; however, by the same token, ensure that you're making yourself visible and heard as often as possible. Demonstrate that you're still a living, breathing entity. There are always things that you can do on social networking platforms to make sure you're staying active.

Even in those circumstances in which you cannot find the motivation to post, but you have already committed to making a certain number of posts for your audience per week, it's always best to communicate directly with your audience about what they would like to see. Ask them if they would prefer seeing a few shorter pieces of content or one longer piece of content covering a major topic for that week. Providing your audience with a say in the content creation process can help them feel more personally invested with the material that they're viewing, in the same way that asking for user feedback in the development process of your MVP forges a relationship between user and product (Chapter 5).

Context

In every post that you make, do your utmost to provide context around it. Merriam-Webster defines context as the 'parts of a discourse that surround a passage and can throw light on its meaning.' In other words, in order for your audience to truly understand the message that you're trying to convey in your content, you need to provide some background that will explain why your message applies to them in their situation. For instance, if you're someone who loves blockchain, the chances of people immediately seeing blockchain and wanting to click in is not as likely as if they saw a general statement first like, 'How much do you understand about your financial situation?' which then proceeds into your explanation of blockchain. The key is to hook people into your posts by providing general context around what you're talking about from the start. This will allow viewers to better visualize the topic through your frame of reference, making the content more persuasive and vivid overall. When providing context, you should intend to be specific, so that you're clearing up any possible misinterpretations that may arise. Giving context in written content is executed slightly differently. According to Julien Samson of writingcooperative.com, you can provide context in your written content through any of the following ways: details about yourself or character, a backstory, explaining an environment, a life-changing situation, a memory, an anecdote, among others. These examples of context can help to create a relationship between the reader and your personal brand, as there is a high probability that someone out there can relate to the context you have given.[1] As a general rule, you should limit the context that you provide in your writing to a paragraph, or perhaps 20 seconds maximum in a video, so that you're not veering away from your central message. The importance of context can be detailed in a comparison with content by author Ngaruiya Githegi, which states, 'content is what you *make* for them. Context is what you *mean* to them.'

Collaboration

You will eventually reach a point when you realize that social media growth, as a means of developing your personal brand, cannot be achieved alone. Part of this may be because you cannot muster up new ideas for content, but another major reason why most creators collaborate is because it can be very enjoyable for all parties. Make it your mission to search for other people to work with in order to put your content out. If you're on LinkedIn, find other people that use LinkedIn and post content daily. Film a video with them, write an article with them, make a post about them going over their profile. An increasingly popular method of collaboration among creators on platforms like YouTube and LinkedIn (shorter clips can also be distributed on other platforms as well) is conducting an interview series in the form of a regular podcast. Interviews are an effective way to connect with those you want to network with. You get to invite guests who you believe will be of interest to both you and your audience, and they're able to share their ideas and perspectives about a topic related to their expertise. One of the most attractive aspects of this interview series is that you can provide your guest with value by giving them something tangible for their precious time, which they can also turn into content for their personal page. This can serve as a launching point for a relationship with this individual moving forward.

Quantity vs quality

There is always a trade-off that many content creators face in relation to the consistency of their content output. This is the debate between **quantity** versus **quality**. To tackle this issue, you must realize that first and foremost, you have to be proud of the content that you're putting out. The fastest way that creators lose motivation to post is when they don't see the purpose of their own work. You must have an innate satisfaction with the content that you produce, regardless of the engagement that it yields. A misconception many people have is that if you're producing several pieces of content within a short span of time (a day or week), you're automatically bringing a lack of effort to each piece. This is not necessarily the case, and if you feel that this applies to you, question whether or not you're being overly critical of your work.

A response to this can be found in a quote from Gary Vaynerchuck: 'A lack of consistency is a massive vulnerability.' When we are too deeply concerned with perfection, we are using time that could instead be dedicated to allowing the audience to live with our content. You may miss out on the right opportunity to speak about a popular current issue because you're committed to making your content flawless.

How can you give back to the larger ecosystem?

You have finally built this personal brand and social media following that you have worked so hard for. The next step is just as – if not more – necessary than the points above, and that is to forward pay what you have learned (which will directly help build your platform). Go visit your local high school and provide mentorship for students there. Teach them your knowledge of the fundamentals of starting your own business and growing a personal brand. You can also look into hosting meetups in your local area, for budding entrepreneurs and people who have an interest in the space that you're in. In 2016, Swish helped organize the first LinkedIn Local, with the purpose of bringing together social networks in an offline setting within your area. By facilitating events like this (which can easily be done by contacting the LinkedIn team directly), you will be responsible for other people expanding their network and meeting individuals that they may not have met otherwise, which is a gratifying feeling. If you don't have the time to organize a meetup, you can simply attend them to share your knowledge with others. Facebook and LinkedIn are the best platforms to search for meetups in your proximity.

Another way in which you can pay it forward is by supporting other startups that pique your interest. Thus far in his career, Swish has invested in several companies including Smile Innovations Group and FazeClan. Investing capital is a great way of giving back when you're willing to provide money towards projects that you care about, but don't yet have the time to directly contribute to in another fashion.

Investing in startups can be done through platforms like Kickstarter, GoFundMe, and AngelList, among others. Another way that Swish has been able to pay his knowledge and expertise forward is by publicly speaking at events, through keynote presentations and panel discussions. He speaks quite a bit about entrepreneurship and building Surf over the last two years. He does this primarily at colleges and universities and shares his advice with students on how they can network better, start a company while in school, and effectively create a personal brand. Swish has also appeared on many podcasts and interview shows and created his own interview series on LinkedIn. Part of what he loves to do is pay his thoughts forward. Not just any and all of his thoughts – his personal brand has been built around the stuff in this book. These are the things he's dealing with and learning, so these are the things he's thinking about day to day... so these are the things he talks about! Whether it's personal branding, starting a business, or networking, what he has to say relates back to his own experience. Now, he has more ways to talk to people than ever before, but the theme is always the same.

He started with this: when you figure something out, *don't just keep it to yourself.* You don't have to have a huge platform to start with: look at meetups, support groups, investing, or speaking opportunities as ways to give back and pay your knowledge forward. That is a core responsibility we want to give to people who are reading this book – and who knows, while you're paying it forward, you might just gain some customers. So take these insights, use them well... and then pass them on!

How is the ecosystem going to change in the future?

Worldwide entrepreneurial ecosystems are bound to experience change in the upcoming years. There are two key ways that the ecosystem will change in the future: virtual meetings will become the norm, and intrapreneurship will exist.

In some organizations, there are people within management and employees who are not fans of in-person meetings. Sometimes meetings run behind schedule and other times they're unnecessarily elongated to fill the allocated amount of time. Some employees feel that their voice is not heard, and the meeting is typically dominated by a few extroverted figures in leadership positions. Research in a 2017 *Harvard Business Review* article suggests that meetings have lengthened over the past 50 years and that on average, 'executives spend nearly 23 hours a week in them'.[2] With this in mind and taking into consideration what has happened post Covid-19, we believe that the future of business ecosystems is one that involves the least amount of in-person meetings possible. Virtual meetings (conducted over Zoom, Google Hangouts, etc) and webinars will continue to grow in popularity. What we will continue to discover is that these virtual meetings are becoming increasingly in demand because of the location flexibility that they provide employees. Productivity is a huge buzzword among companies, and if employees are feeling less productive after in-person meetings, better alternatives will definitely be implemented.

The second-largest change that will occur within the ecosystem in the future is that more and more corporations will enable intrapreneurship to take place. Intrapreneurship is described as a system that encourages employees to behave like entrepreneurs under a regular company or organization.[3] Like an entrepreneur, an employee will be allowed to take initiative in managing innovative projects, being self-motivated, and taking action when they see justifiable opportunity on the horizon. In part due to the glamorization of entrepreneurs, corporations are beginning to take notice that not only do their employees want to pursue their own work, but they can also be more productive and creative when executing on their own visualized projects. This is exemplified by the story of WeChat, the Chinese multipurpose app that has become one of the world's largest singular mobile apps, with more than 1.25 billion active monthly users.[4] The app was created as a project at Tencent Guangzhou Research and Project Center in 2010. It has now ballooned into China's biggest social network, and the founding company Tencent, an internet-based platform company started in 1998, with stakes in popular video games like Fortnite and Player Unknown Battlegrounds (PUBG), has been able to accumulate billions of dollars as a result of this project that it decided to undertake. Today, WeChat stands as one of the company's primary sources of revenue. Perhaps Snapchat CEO Evan Spiegel explained it best when he commented on WeChat's prominence: 'Tencent very early on understood the power of communication because it drives frequency… if you can be the service that's most frequently used on someone's phone, you're able to develop a lot of other ancillary businesses around that engagement'.[5]

For students in particular, it's important to understand that entrepreneurial ecosystems will not just be effective for entrepreneurs who drop out of school and are pursuing entrepreneurship as a full-time career. As this concept of intrapreneurship becomes more and more popular, corporations will provide more opportunity for employees to innovate and take on these creative freedoms in their work.

There are two other factors to remember when considering how the entrepreneurial ecosystem will change in the future. Number one, there is no 'age' to be an entrepreneur. There are more and more young individuals coming into entrepreneurship, as well as older people – people over 55 and 60 creating their first company.[6] Understand that the spectrum of people who are going to enter into starting their own company will only increase: there are going to be *more people doing it*, so the ecosystem that you might be dominant in right now may not look the same four to five years from now. You should always strive to meet new people and stay on your toes.

Secondly, technology is not the only aspect of entrepreneurship. Although we're mostly working in the tech space, what we've talked about in this book can be applied across industries and sectors – the entrepreneurial ecosystem also contains people who are social entrepreneurs, people who create charities or social ventures. Largely, the principles of creating a business (whether it's a non-profit, for-profit, or a social venture) are relatively the same, especially in the first three years. You want to be connecting and learning from all kinds of entrepreneurs, especially if they're successful.

Notes

1 Samson, J (2017) Why context matters in writing, *Medium*, https://writingcooperative.com/why-context-matters-in-writing-f52ad075c07a (archived at https://perma.cc/F383-FL6Y)

2 Perlow, LA et al (2017) Stop the meeting madness, *Harvard Business Review*, https://hbr.org/2017/07/stop-the-meeting-madness (archived at https://perma.cc/GB35-5EY8)

3 Kenton, W (2020) Intrapreneurship, *Investopedia*, https://www.investopedia.com/terms/i/intrapreneurship.asp (archived at https://perma.cc/67CS-ACVS)

4 Statista (2021) WeChat: active users worldwide, https://www.statista.com/statistics/255778/number-of-active-wechat-messenger-accounts/ (archived at https://perma.cc/Z5TA-EYYM)

5 Brennan, M (2018) One billion users and counting – what's behind WeChat's success? *China Channel*, https://chinachannel.co/one-billion-users-and-counting-whats-behind-wechats-success/ (archived at https://perma.cc/B8JZ-MHST)

6 Paul, JWR (2019) It's never too late: entrepreneurship has no age, *Entrepreneur*, https://www.entrepreneur.com/article/332016 (archived at https://perma.cc/YW5M-BL5V)

INDEX

NB: page numbers in *italic* indicate figures or tables

Printed in the USA
CPSIA information can be obtained
at www.ICGtesting.com
LVHW050800211123
764500LV00040B/1276